The Dead And The Dying

Colors by Val Staples

CRIMINAL VOL. 3: THE DEAD AND THE DYING. Contains material originally published in magazine form as CRIMINAL Vol 2 #1-3. First printing 2008. ISBN# 978-0-7851-3227-1. Published by MARVEL PUBLISHING. INC., a subsidiary of MARVEL ENTERTAINMENT INC. OFFICE OF PUBLICATION: 417 5th Avenue, New York, NY 10016.

Printed in Canada.

10 9 8 7 6 5 4 3 2 1

The Dead and the Dying

A **CRIMINAL** edition by Ed Brubaker and Sean Phillips

Introduction

Life is full of guilty pleasures. Most people are naturally given to heathendom, but few are brave enough to act on the forbidden things we are fascinated by in pop culture... wild sex... violence in its many forms... drug use that would derail our hum drum lives. CRIMINAL is a peephole into this kind of world.

What Ed Brubaker and Sean Phillips have created in this series of books is a world that feels like a 40's/50's film noir or gangster movie, but populated by the children of the 70's blaxploitation and grind-house pictures. But to their credit they've done much more than create a series influenced by other mediums. Brubaker and Phillips have made this seedy atmosphere... personal. It's very hard to create a work with characters that you are alternately repulsed by, yet another part of you feels their pain and emotions. The characters in CRIMINAL are victims of their own fate, a path that doesn't seem to come from the mind of Brubaker as much as it seems organic to the nature of the world they live and breathe in.

This volume of CRIMINAL, the *Dead and the Dying*, takes place in the years 1967 to 1973, during the height of the Vietnam War. This was a period where the nation fought an internal battle against our past and possible future. We were in the middle of a fucking civil war and didn't even know it. This was a time where the rules changed. The social conventions of old didn't hold. Black and White people were making connections on levels never seen previously. And with this... the STREETS evolved as well.

Some folks turned to smack to escape the world around them. The streets, which always had its share of seedy types, were suddenly filled with newcomers to the underworld. Movies of this era like *Point Blank* and *Across 110th Street* explored this world, but what Brubaker and Phillips have done is much more radical. They have created a multiethnic cesspool of characters that are all barely hanging onto their sanity. All the folks in CRIMINAL, even the supporting characters, are on the hustle, looking for the next score... and no one is above blowing someone's head off or fucking to get what they want.

In CRIMINAL, there in no law save for the RULE OF THE STREETS. Crooks lay the foundations here, cops exist in the background and a man's rep is the most important thing to him. Strange stories emerge from this milieu. Guys come back from Vietnam killers and show what they learned in the jungle right here in the streets. An idealistic pretty black girl can fall for a rich white boy and have her whole life turned upside down. And a black man can grow up the son of a progressive gangster, attempt to avoid his father's path and still find the road to ruin.

I love how these self-contained stories each show another piece of a larger picture, focusing on someone who seemed like a side character in the previous part.

How Sean Phillips figures out with a pen how to hit the right emotional beat and cast a character's face in shadow on the right line, I don't know, but it's pure fucking genius. He and Brubaker take us a to another place and we are like voyeurs to a world that none of us would want to live in. It's dangerous, seedy and sexy... and you know what? We dig it.

And who else but Ed Brubaker would come up with the line "MY PUSSY WAS A DEADY WEAPON" and we not only laugh, but still take the character seriously? Brubaker is winning with CRIMINAL because he alternates the brutality of these characters with vulnerability and heart. The end result makes them more human, and forcing us to feel this way serves up discomfort and delight.

Thanks for the stress, Ed. Keep the stories coming.

John Singleton
June 4, 2008

John Singleton is the award-winning writer/director of BOYZ N THE HOOD, ROSEWOOD, SHAFT and many more.

SECOND CHANCE IN HELL

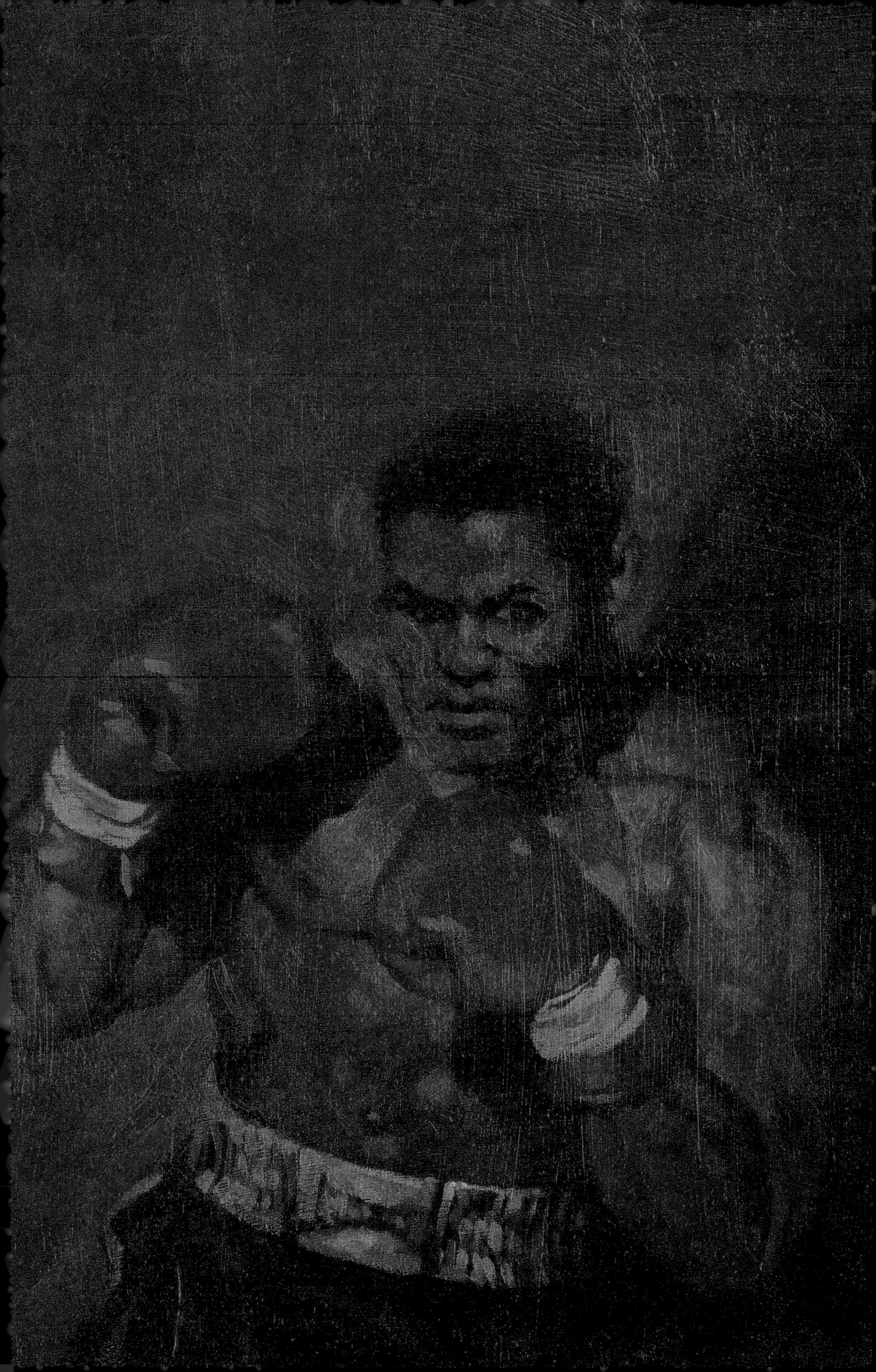

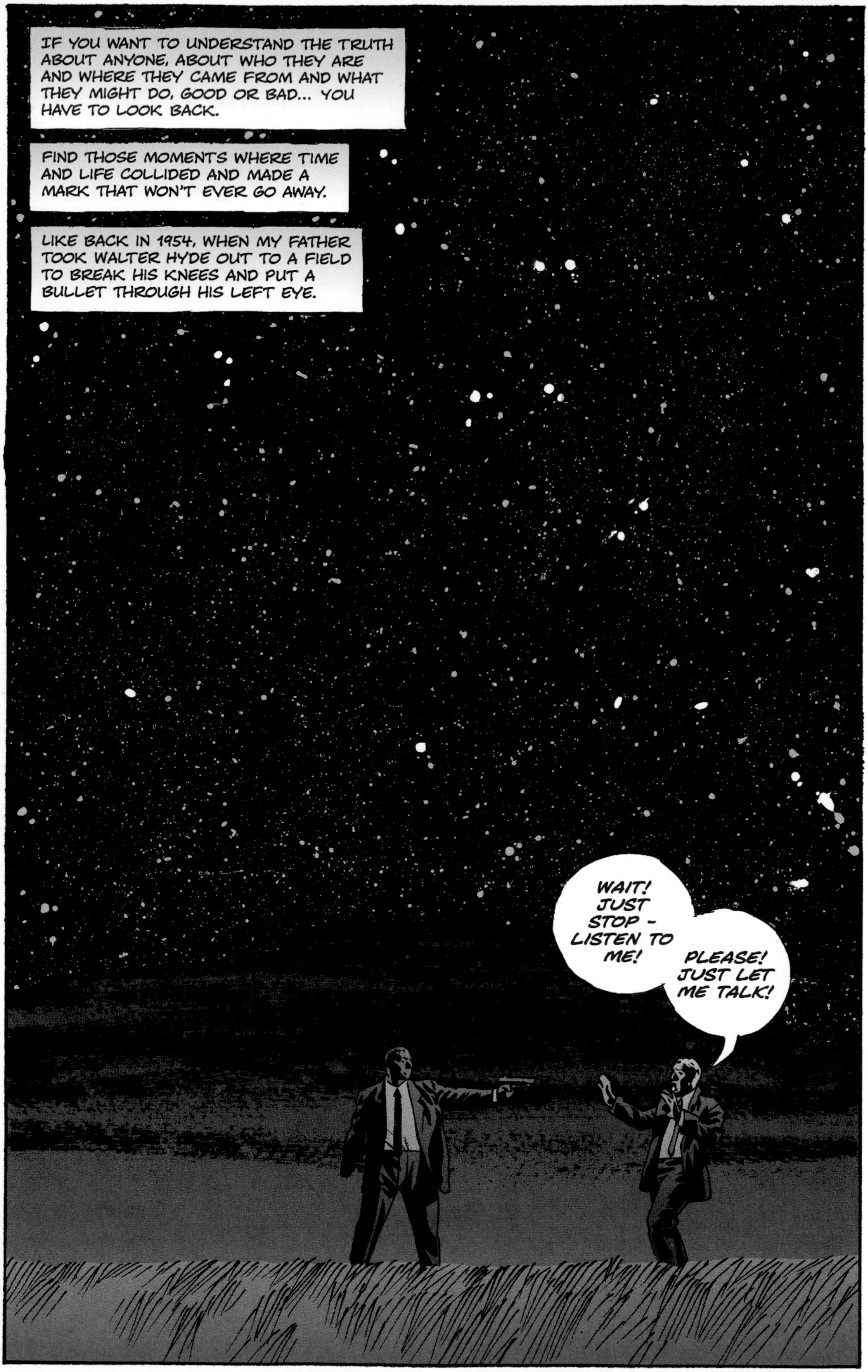
IF YOU WANT TO UNDERSTAND THE TRUTH ABOUT ANYONE, ABOUT WHO THEY ARE AND WHERE THEY CAME FROM AND WHAT THEY MIGHT DO, GOOD OR BAD... YOU HAVE TO LOOK BACK.
FIND THOSE MOMENTS WHERE TIME AND LIFE COLLIDED AND MADE A MARK THAT WON'T EVER GO AWAY.
LIKE BACK IN 1954, WHEN MY FATHER TOOK WALTER HYDE OUT TO A FIELD TO BREAK HIS KNEES AND PUT A BULLET THROUGH HIS LEFT EYE.
WAIT! JUST STOP - LISTEN TO ME!
PLEASE! JUST LET ME TALK!

THERE WASN'T ONE GOOD REASON IN THE WORLD HE SHOULDN'T HAVE DONE HIS JOB THAT NIGHT.

CLEVON! LISTEN TO ME!

BUT IN THEIR OWN WAY, THE HYDES HAVE ALWAYS BEEN LUCKY.

AND DAD LIKED WALTER... BUT HE'D KILLED PLENTY OF MEN HE LIKED.

C'MON, WALT... YOU KNOW THE SCORE.

IT WASN'T FOR A BLACK MAN TO MAKE THOSE CHOICES, NOT BACK THEN. NOT IN MY FATHER'S WORLD.

BUT YOU AND ME – WE'RE DIFFERENT!

DON'T DO THIS!

AND YET...

ALL RIGHT... TALK.

WHATTA YOU GOT TO SAY'S GONNA CHANGE A THING?

AS IT TURNED OUT, WHAT WALTER HYDE SAID NEXT CHANGED EVERYTHING.

HE LAID OUT A VISION FOR THE FUTURE, WITH A PLACE IN IT FOR MY FATHER BEYOND ANYTHING HE'D EVER THOUGHT POSSIBLE.

OVER THE NEXT TWO WEEKS, WALTER HYDE AND CLEVON BROWN TOOK OUT THE OLD GUARD ONE BY ONE.

IT WAS A HOUSE-CLEANING.

A BLOODY COUP THAT LEFT NO ONE STANDING IN HYDE'S WAY.

NO ONE TO STOP HIM FROM TAKING OVER ALL THE SYNDICATE BUSINESS IN THE CITY AND CHANGING THE WAY THAT BUSINESS WAS CONDUCTED.

HYDE WENT RIGHT FROM MID-LEVEL LIEUTENANT TO TOP BOSS WHEN MOST OF HIS ENEMIES THOUGHT HE WAS ALREADY DEAD, AND MY FATHER MADE THAT POSSIBLE.

AS A REWARD, HE BECAME WALTER HYDE'S RIGHT-HAND MAN.

OFFICIALLY, HE WAS HIS DRIVER, HIS BODYGUARD, AND HIS ENFORCER

UNOFFICIALLY, HE WAS HIS CLOSEST ADVISOR.

THAT'S HOW MY FAMILY ENDED UP MOVING TO THE *HYDE ESTATE* WHEN I WAS FOUR YEARS OLD...

...AND HOW A BLACK KID IN THE 1950S GREW UP WITH A RICH WHITE KID NAMED *SEBASTIAN HYDE* FOR A BEST FRIEND.

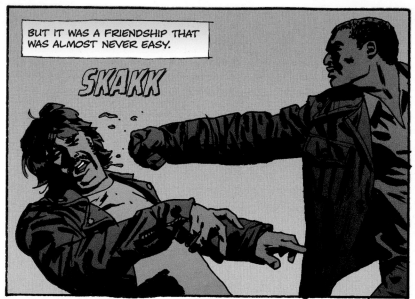

BUT IT WAS A FRIENDSHIP THAT WAS ALMOST NEVER EASY.

SKAKK

1972

HIT HIM **AGAIN**.

HE KNOWS HE'S BEEN HIT.

YOU KNOW THAT, DON'T YA?

...YEAH... YEAH... NO MORE...

WHATTA YOU GOT TO **SAY** TO THE MAN, THEN?

I'M – I'M **SORRY!**

WON'T BE NO MORE SKIMMIN'... I **SWEAR** TO CHRIST!

ON MY **FUCKIN' GRAVE!**

IT **WILL** BE YOUR GRAVE, SCUTTER, IF THIS SHIT GOES ON **ONE MORE TIME.**

I HEAR YOU... I SWEAR..

THANKS, JAKE... I DIDN'T KNOW WHO ELSE TO CALL.

NOT WITHOUT MY *DAD* FINDING OUT.

I KNOW, BUT... YOU CAN'T BE DOING THIS TO ME NO MORE.

SHIT LIKE THIS, ANYONE *HEARS* ABOUT IT... THIS COULD COST ME EVERYTHING.

GOT A CAREER ON THE LINE NOW.

THIS AIN'T LIKE THE OLD DAYS.

I *KNOW*... YOU THINK I DON'T KNOW THAT?

WHO THE HELL DO YOU THINK IS *PAYING* FOR ALL THAT AND SETTING UP ALL THOSE BOUTS?

AND TAKIN' A *HEALTHY CUT* OF MY *WINNINGS*?

THAT'D BE *YOUR DAD*.

I'M SERIOUS, *SEBASTIAN*, DON'T BE CALLIN' ME FOR MUSCLE.

I CAN'T BE THAT GUY.

AW, C'MON JAKE... IT'S *US*.

I GOTTA GO TRAIN... I'LL SEEYA LATER ON.

SEBASTIAN HAD BEEN HOME FROM COLLEGE FOR ALMOST A YEAR, TAKING THE FIRST STEPS TOWARDS INHERITING HIS FATHER'S EMPIRE.

I'D GONE PRO A WHILE BEFORE THAT, AND WAS DOING REAL WELL FOR MYSELF.

THIRTEEN BOUTS, NO LOSSES. EIGHT KOS, FIVE DECISIONS.

I'D DONE SO WELL THAT MY MANAGER, TWEEDY, HAD DECIDED TO MOVE ME UP TO HEAVYWEIGHT.

BEFORE MY FATHER SUCCUMBED TO HIS CANCER, HE'D MADE WALTER HYDE PROMISE TO TAKE CARE OF WHATEVER I NEEDED.

AND I GOT THE FEELING AS LONG AS I KEPT WINNING, THAT PROMISE WOULD BE KEPT.

OTHERWISE, IT HAD BEEN SOME TIME SINCE HYDE FOUND ME ANYTHING BUT AN ANNOYANCE AND A BAD INFLUENCE ON HIS SON.

SO, IMAGINE MY SURPRISE WHEN I SEE THE PRIME REASON FOR THE OLD MAN'S CONTEMPT FOR ME STAGGERING DOWN FAYETTE STREET THAT MORNING...

...LOOKING LIKE SHE HADN'T SLEPT IN DAYS.

I SHOULD HAVE GONE ACROSS THE STREET... SAID SOMETHING. BUT I'M ASHAMED TO SAY I JUST TURNED AWAY.

IT WAS A BAD ENOUGH DAY ALREADY, WHY MAKE IT WORSE?

BUT IT GOT WORSE ANYWAY. SOME THINGS ARE JUST LIKE THAT.

AND DANICA BRIGGS WAS ONE OF THOSE THINGS.

SHE GOT RIGHT IN MY HEAD AND GNAWED AT ME ALL THROUGH MY WORK-OUT.

NO! NO NO NO!

THE HELL'RE YOU *DOIN'*, GNARLY?

WE DON'T PAY MELVIN TO WHALE ON YER BLACK ASS.

YER S'POSED TO WHALE ON *HIS!*

AIN'T THAT RIGHT, MELVIN?

IT USUALLY *DOES* GO THAT WAY, MR TWEEDY.

I'M SORRY, TWEED... MY HEAD'S ALL OVER THE PLACE TODAY.

WELL, GO MAKE IT RIGHT, THEN...

LAST THING I NEED IS YOU GETTIN' *HURT* BEFORE THE FIGHT NEXT WEEK.

DANICA. ONCE I SAW HER I COULDN'T LET IT GO.

I WANTED TO. A BIG PART OF ME WANTED TO.

BUT I OWED HER SOMETHING AND I NEVER HAVE CARRIED DEBTS TOO WELL.

SHE WASN'T CHECKED IN AT THE *RED ROBIN,* AT LEAST NOT UNDER HER OWN NAME.

WHAT I LOOK LIKE, INFORMATION SERVICE TO YOU?

SO I COMBED THE LOCAL BARS, FIGURING SHE'D BE AT ONE.

AND I FIGURED RIGHT.

SHE WAS WAITING TABLES AT THE UNDERTOWN, AN OLD SPEAKEASY THAT HAD NEVER QUITE GONE LEGIT.

HAMSUNN, THE CURRENT OWNER, WAS AN EX-THIEF AND A REAL BASTARD.

AND IT LOOKED LIKE HE AND DANICA WERE PRETTY COZY. I TRIED TO IGNORE THAT.

SO, JAKE "GNARLY" BROWN... WHAT THE HELL ARE *YOU* SUPPOSED TO BE?

SOME BIG BOXING CHAMP NOW?

DANICA... IT'S BEEN A LONG TIME.

UH HUNH. YOU *ORDERING?*

NO. I'M IN TRAINING. I WAS HOPING WE COULD *TALK.*

NOTHIN' TO TALK ABOUT, MAN.

YOU AIN'T DRINKIN', YOU BEST CLEAR THIS BOOTH.

WAIT. I WANTED TO...

WHAT?!

TO HELP... IF...

THINK I HAD **ENOUGH** HELP FROM YOU, JAKE.

DAMN. WOULD YOU JUST SIT DOWN AND BE **REAL** FOR ONE MINUTE?

THIS IS AS REAL AS IT GETS.

NOW GET YER FUCKIN' HAND OFF ME.

WE GOT A **PROBLEM** HERE?

NO PROBLEM, BABY...

YOU WANT TO PUT THAT BAT DOWN, OLD MAN. NOW.

AN' YOU WANNA GET OUTTA MY BAR NOW.

MAY BE A BIG MAN IN THE RING, BUT NOT IN HERE.

YOU AIN'T'CHER DADDY... **BOY.**

THAT WORD JUST HANGS THERE, LIKE A DEATH THREAT.

I TELL MYSELF FOR THE SECOND TIME TODAY THAT I HAVE TOO MUCH TO LOSE.

AND I STOP BEFORE I DO SOMETHING I'M GONNA REGRET.

BUT REGRET IS ALL I HAVE ONCE I HIT THE STREETS. MEMORIES AND REGRETS.

AREN'T THEY THE SAME THING?

I MET DANICA BRIGGS BACK IN 1967.

SHE WAS A FRIEND OF TWEEDY'S GRAND-DAUGHTER, AND THEY LIKED TO HANG AROUND THE GYM.

I KNEW RIGHT AWAY THERE WAS SOMETHING SPECIAL ABOUT THIS ONE. SOMETIMES YOU JUST DO.

SHE WAS SMARTER AND FUNNIER – *BOLDER* -- THAN ANY GIRL I'D EVER SEEN BEFORE.

I THINK THAT WAS THE FIRST TIME I EVER KNEW HEARTBREAK, JUST LISTENING TO THAT GIRL'S LAUGH.

OF COURSE THE REAL HEARTBREAK CAME LATER, WHEN SEBASTIAN FELL FOR HER EVEN HARDER THAN I HAD.

AND I STEPPED ASIDE FOR HIM.

MAYBE IT WAS THE LOOK SHE GOT ON HER FACE WHEN SHE KNEW THE RICHEST KID IN TOWN WANTED HER.

OR MAYBE I JUST FELT I OWED SEBASTIAN. HIS DAD HAD PULLED A LOT OF STRINGS TO GET US BOTH PASSED OVER IN THE DRAFT.

BUT IF I'D JUST STEPPED UP, SO MUCH COULD HAVE BEEN DIFFERENT.

SEBASTIAN WOULDN'T HAVE BEEN SENT AWAY TO COLLEGE. DANICA WOULDN'T HAVE BEEN HURT SO BAD.

AND I WOULDN'T STILL BE HEARING HER VOICE THAT DAY BEFORE SHE LEFT.

CRYING ABOUT WHAT THEY'D DONE TO HER. BLAMING ME.

DID YOU HEAR ABOUT *SCUTTER*?

NO... WHAT IS IT *THIS* TIME?

HE GOT KILLED.

THEY FOUND HIM LATE LAST NIGHT... SHOT IN THE BACK, ALL HIS FINGERS CUT OFF.

JESUS.

YEAH. DAD HAS PEOPLE REPORTING BACK TO HIM ABOUT MY BUSINESS.

PEOPLE WHO *SUPPOSEDLY* WORK FOR *ME*.

WELL, YOU *WANTED* THAT WORLD, MAN...

IS *THAT* HOW I GOT HERE? 'CAUSE I FORGET SOMETIMES *WHO* WANTED *WHAT*.

Y'KNOW... THE ONE THING MY DAD ALWAYS DRUMMED INTO ME IS THAT WE *DON'T* HAVE TO GROW UP TO BE OUR FATHERS.

SURE, BUT IN YOUR CASE THAT'S *A GOOD THING*.

NO, I MEAN -- NOTHING AGAINST *CLEVON*... BUT TIMES HAVE *CHANGED*, JAKE...

A BLACK MAN HAS DIFFERENT OPPORTUNITIES NOW THAN *HE* DID.

AND YOU'RE SO FAMILIAR WITH THE PLIGHT OF THE *BLACK MAN*, HUNH?

HEY, I SAW *SHAFT*.

LOOK, SEBASTIAN, WE *BOTH* KNOW WHAT'S GOIN' ON. YOUR DAD WANTS YOU TO PROVE HOW *TOUGH* YOU ARE.

AND TO HIM TOUGH AND *MEAN* ARE THE SAME THING.

YOU HAVE THAT *IN YOU*? YOU *READY* TO BE MEAN?

WHAT DO *YOU* THINK?

I THINK YOU *WANNA* BE.

I THINK YOU BEEN WANTIN' TO BE MEAN AS A *SON OF A BITCH* FOR YEARS.

I ALMOST TOLD SEBASTIAN ABOUT DANICA BEING BACK THAT DAY...

BUT SOMETHING INSIDE WOULDN'T LET ME.

SHE WAS SOMETHING WE HADN'T TALKED ABOUT FOR YEARS.

NOT SINCE THE NIGHT WHEN I FIRST SAW REAL HATE IN SEBASTIAN'S EYES.

BEFORE THAT, WE'D BEEN BROTHERS, OF A STRANGE SORT.

EACH OUT OF PLACE IN THE OTHER'S WORLD, BUT FEARLESS ABOUT IT.

SO I HAD THOUGHT.

BUT I DIDN'T TRUST HIM ANYMORE. NOT LIKE I WANTED TO.

I JUST TRUSTED HE'D DO THE WRONG THING.

HEY, JACKIE... YOU KNOW YOUR OLD *FRIEND'S* BACK IN TOWN?

GNARLY... YOU BEST STAY *CLEAR* OF THAT GIRL.

SHE *AIN'T* WHAT SHE USED TO BE.

SHE AIN'T NO GOOD.

JUST TELL ME WHERE SHE *STAYS*, JACKIE. SAVE THE LECTURE.

IF I DIDN'T ALREADY KNOW TWEEDY'S GRANDDAUGHTER WAS *RIGHT*, I WOULD'VE WHEN I SAW *WHERE* DANICA WAS LIVING.

THE CADENHEAD WAS ONE OF THE MOST EXPENSIVE HOTELS IN TOWN.

NOT A PLACE A WAITRESS COULD AFFORD.

-AFRAID MISS BRIGGS IS *OUT*. WOULD YOU LIKE TO LEAVE A NOTE?

NAH... THAT'S ALL RIGHT.

LIFE IS FULL OF IFS.

IF ONLY I'D SAID *THIS*... IF ONLY I'D *DONE THAT*.

IF NOT FOR MY GUILTY CONSCIENCE, I WOULDN'T HAVE WAITED FOR HER.

IF NOT FOR THE RAIN...

I WOULDN'T HAVE FOUND OUT I WASN'T THE *ONLY ONE* KEEPING SECRETS.

IF NOT FOR MY ANGER, I WOULDN'T HAVE COUNTED THE LONG MINUTES SEBASTIAN WAS IN HER HOTEL ROOM...

...BEFORE HE HURRIED HOME. BACK TO DADDY'S MANSION.

PROBLEM IS, ALL THE IFS IN THE WORLD NEVER MAKE A DAMN BIT OF DIFFERENCE.

KNK KNKK

HOLD ON... I AIN'T -

9

--DECENT...

SHIT.

9

YOU JUST DON'T KNOW WHEN TO SAY WHEN, DO YA?

WHAT THE HELL'RE YOU DOIN', DANICA?

9 9

YOU WON'T EVEN TALK TO ME, BUT YOU'RE BALLIN' HIM?

AFTER EVERYTHING?

THIS SHIT IS REALLY NONE OF YOUR BUSINESS, MAN.

'SIDES, I THOUGHT SEBASTIAN WAS YOUR BUDDY?

DON'T DO THAT. THIS ISN'T ABOUT THAT.

ISN'T IT? ISN'T HE A STAND-UP GUY?

ISN'T THAT WHAT YOU TOLD ME?

WHY CAN'T YOU JUST LEAVE ME BE, JAKE?

I JUST DON'T WANT YOU TO GET *HURT*, DANICA.

LET ME WORRY ABOUT *ME*, CHAMP... *OKAY?*

I DON'T HURT SO *EASY* ANYMORE...

NOT AFTER THEY RIPPED ME UP LIKE THEY DONE.

SEBASTIAN'S *NOT* WHO HE USED TO BE... IT ISN'T *SAFE* AROUND HIM.

SHIT, IT NEVER *WAS*... WAS IT?

...I'M JUST... *SO* SORRY...

THAT'S... THAT'S *SWEET*, REALLY...

BUT YOU DON'T GOT NOTHIN' TO BE SORRY FOR.

IT'S A KISS THAT'S FIVE YEARS TOO LATE.

IT TASTES LIKE ASHES AND TEARS. LIKE A GOODBYE KISS.

WHICH IS WHAT IT IS.

I SPEND THE NEXT TWO WEEKS TRYING TO FORGET THAT NIGHT, AND OBSESSING OVER EVERY DETAIL OF IT AT THE SAME TIME.

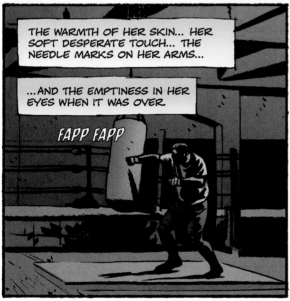

THE WARMTH OF HER SKIN... HER SOFT DESPERATE TOUCH... THE NEEDLE MARKS ON HER ARMS...

...AND THE EMPTINESS IN HER EYES WHEN IT WAS OVER

FAPP FAPP

I TRY TO WASH IT ALL OUT OF MY MIND, TRAINING LIKE CRAZY FOR MY NEXT BOUT, WITH AN ACTUAL *CONTENDER* THIS TIME.

IT DOESN'T WORK, I *STILL* OBSESS...

FAPP FAPP FAPP

...BUT IT TURNS OUT I'M OBSESSING OVER THE WRONG DETAILS.

MOTHERFUCKERS! FUCK!

HEY... CALM DOWN, MAN...

WHAT THE FUCK?

MY PICK-UP STASH GOT HIT.

I GOT FUCKING *ROBBED.*

TWO GUYS *BUSTED IN* DURING WEEKEND COUNT, ICED MY MEN...

AND TOOK OFF WITH *FIFTY GRAND.* MAYBE MORE.

WHAT'RE YOU GONNA DO?

I'M *FUCKED...* IT'S NOT EVEN THE *MONEY.*

IT'S THE *RESPECT,* Y'KNOW?

MY DAD... YOUR DAD... EVERYTHING THEY *BUILT.*

YOU'RE SOUNDIN' LIKE *WALTER* NOW.

I *AM* HIM, FAR AS THESE STREETS KNOW.

THEY HIT THE *HYDES.*

FFP

WHY ARE YOU BRINGIN' THIS TO *ME,* MAN?

OH, DON'T *WORRY,* I DON'T EXPECT YOU TO GET *INVOLVED...*

SEBASTIAN... *C'MON,* MAN.

HEY, I *KNOW,* OKAY?

NOT YOUR WORLD. I *GET IT.*

BUT I'M GONNA *FIND* THESE FUCKWADS...

AND I'M GONNA DO *EXACTLY* WHAT OUR FATHERS WOULD'VE.

I WONDER HOW LONG IT'LL TAKE HIM TO FIGURE IT OUT, BECAUSE SEBASTIAN *ISN'T* STUPID.

AND THE NEXT DAY, OLD HAMSUNN IS FOUND BEATEN TO DEATH IN THE BACK OF HIS BAR...

SO I KNOW TIME ISN'T ON MY SIDE.

SORRY, SHE HASN'T BEEN *AROUND* TODAY, SIR.

WHY DIDN'T I SEE THIS COMING?

NO, I AIN'T SEEN HER NOT FOR A WHILE.

WHY DID I THINK SHE WAS AFTER ANYTHING BUT REVENGE FROM SEBASTIAN?

AND WHAT BETTER REVENGE THAN TO *SHAME HIM* BEFORE HIS FATHER?

I COMB THE STREETS ALL DAY, WITH NO LUCK...

...PRAYING SHE'S SMART ENOUGH TO BE LONG GONE.

AND SHE IS, JUST NOT HOW I MEANT.

YEAH, THAT'S HER

ANY *REASON* YOU WERE ALL OVER TOWN ASKIN' FOR HER YESTERDAY?

AM I A *SUSPECT?*

NAH...SHE WAS IN HERE THE WHOLE TIME YOU WERE LOOKIN'.

BEEN DEAD SINCE YESTERDAY *MORNIN'.*

NO... SHE WAS DEAD A *LONG TIME* BEFORE THAT.

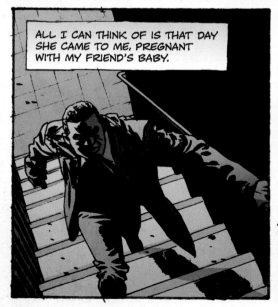

ALL I CAN THINK OF IS THAT DAY SHE CAME TO ME, PREGNANT WITH MY FRIEND'S BABY.

AND HOW I SENT HER TO THE WOLVES.

NOT ON PURPOSE, THOUGH, AND NOT ON MY OWN...

YOU SON OF A BITCH!

WHAT?

YOU GAVE IT *ALL* UP, DIDN'T YOU?!

BACK OFF, JAKE... *BACK OFF.*

TRYIN' TO BE A *BIG MAN*?!

BRAGGIN' WHILE YOU *FUCKED HER*?!

GAVE UP YOUR *OWN* STASH HOUSE, AND DIDN'T EVEN *REALIZE* IT...

JAKE... WALK AWAY FROM ME. *NOW.*

FUCK YOU.

SLAPP

A SLAP. OPEN PALM. NOT EVEN A BACKHAND.

AND WE BOTH KNOW WHAT IT MEANS.

SLAPP

DAD! JESUS!

YOU HONESTLY THINK YOU'RE GONNA *MARRY* THIS BITCH?

I... I...

YOU'RE A *HYDE*, YOU SPOILED LITTLE BRAT.

YOU'RE *NOT* MARRYING THE FIRST LITTLE NIGGER YOU KNOCK UP.

UNDERSTAND ME?

YES... YES SIR...

CLEVON, HAVE SOMEONE TAKE CARE OF THIS GIRL.

SURE, WALT. NO PROBLEM.

GNARLY?

YOU READY TO *FIGHT*, SON?

YEAH, SORRY, TWEEDY... JUST THINKIN'...

WELL, STOP *THAT* NONSENSE, AND LET'S GO KICK SOME TAIL.

I PUT ON THE BEST FIGHT OF MY LIFE THAT NIGHT. LIKE I WAS FIGHTING ALI OR FRAZER.

LIKE I HAD SOMETHING TO PROVE.

AND I DID, BECAUSE THEY'RE WAITING FOR ME THE NEXT NIGHT.

SEBASTIAN'S GUYS. HIS NEW ONES.

I HURT A FEW OF THEM PRETTY BAD... BUT THERE ARE JUST TOO MANY.

A LEAD PIPE PUTS ME DOWN.

THEN THEY BREAK MY LEG IN FOUR PLACES. SHATTER MY KNEECAP.

AND I KNOW I'LL NEVER FIGHT AGAIN.

BUT I KNEW WHAT I WAS DOING WHEN I SHAMED SEBASTIAN HYDE IN PUBLIC...

JESUS...

I KNEW THERE'D BE A PRICE.

... *LOOK* AT YOU.

I CAN'T *BELIEVE* THIS... I DIDN'T WANNA –

DON'T FUCKING *APOLOGIZE* TO ME.

YOU THINK I *WANTED* THIS? OVER SOME *CHICK*?

YOU'RE MY OLDEST FRIEND...

NO. WE *AREN'T* FRIENDS... NOT FOR *YEARS*.

SHE MEANT *THAT MUCH* TO YOU?

WASN'T JUST HER... IT WAS WHAT YOU LET THEM *DO* TO HER

YOU KNOW SHE COULDN'T GET PREGNANT AFTER THAT?

JESUS. I WAS A *KID*... A STUPID FUCKING KID.

AND LOOK WHAT YOU'VE GROWN UP *INTO*...

YOU DON'T **UNDERSTAND**, MAN...

YEAH, I **DO**.

YOUR LIFE WAS ALWAYS A **TRAP**, SEBASTIAN...

YOU HAD **ONE CHANCE** TO GET OUT AND YOU BLEW IT.

AND NOW WE **BOTH** KNOW WHO YOU **REALLY** ARE.

JAKE... C'MON...

DON'T YOU CRY TO ME.

DON'T YOU **EVER** FUCKING CRY AGAIN.

JUST GET THE FUCK OUTTA HERE...

AND THAT'S JUST WHAT HE DID.

HE WENT BACK TO HIS WORLD, WHERE HE EVENTUALLY BECAME ONE OF THE MOST FEARED MEN IN THIS CITY...

...AND I STAYED IN THAT HOSPITAL ROOM, TRYING TO FIGURE OUT WHAT THE HELL TO DO WITH MY LIFE.

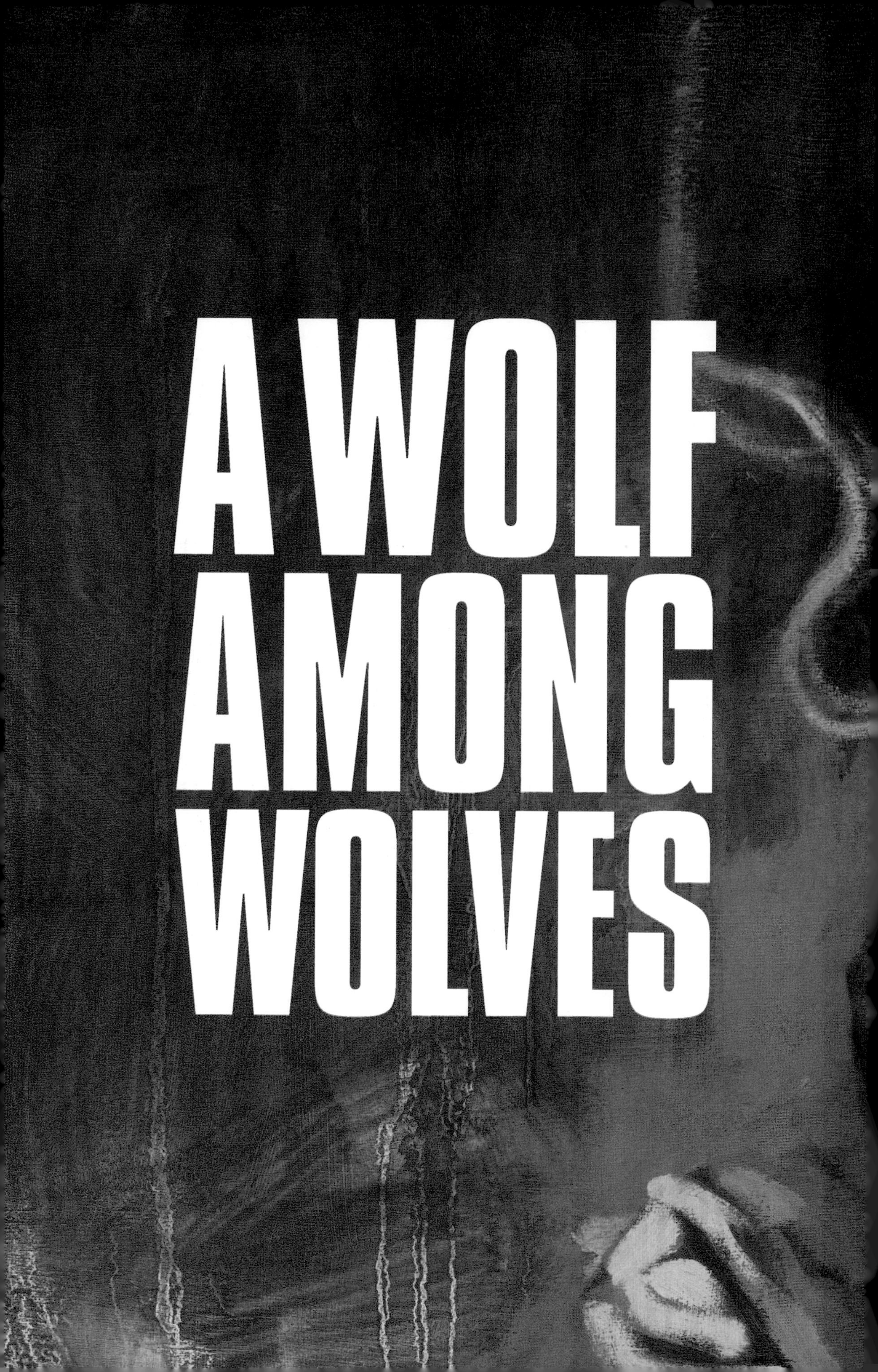
A WOLF
AMONG
WOLVES

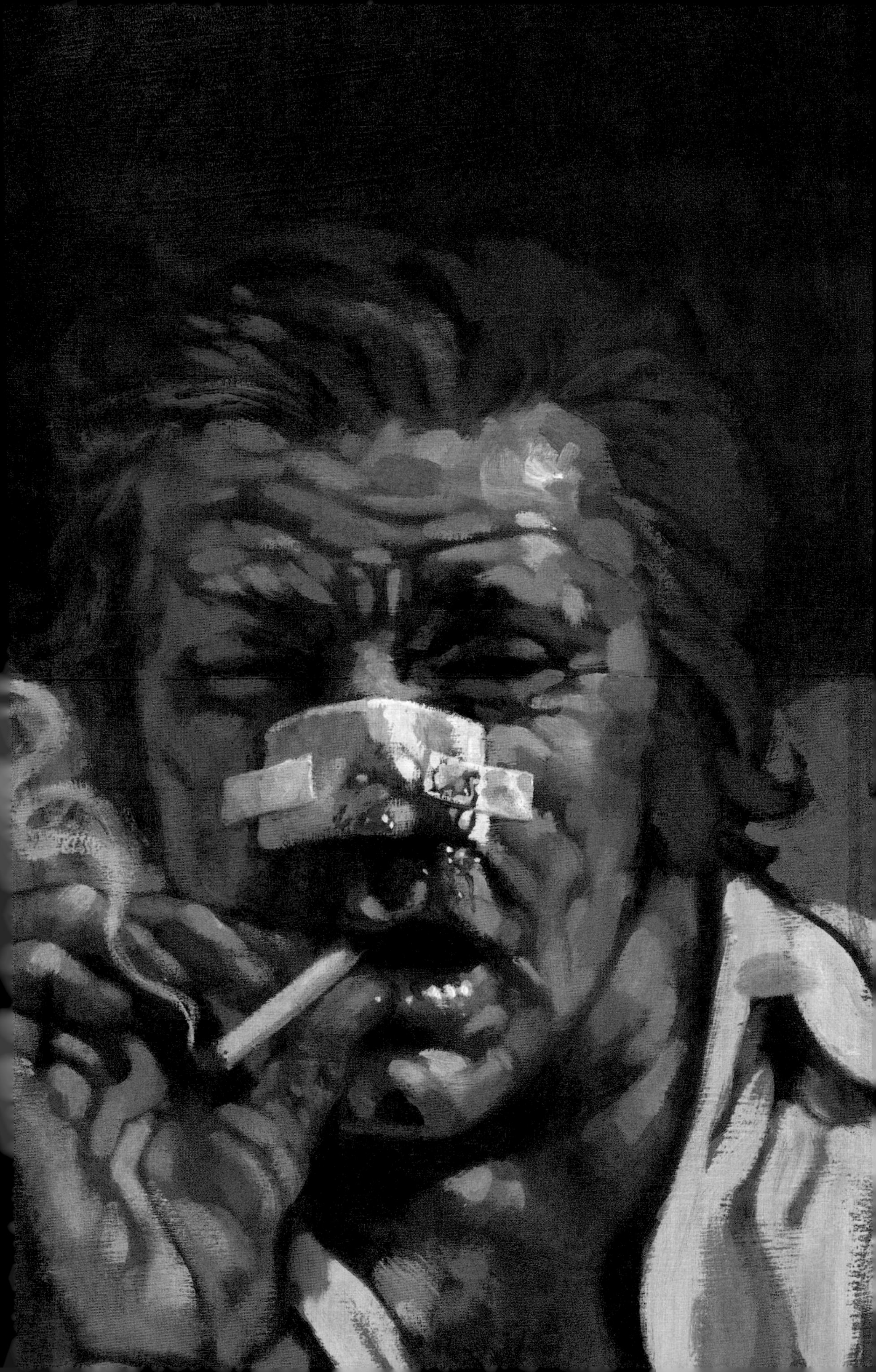

WHEN TEEG LAWLESS CAME HOME IN 1972, HE BROUGHT THE WAR HOME WITH HIM.

AFTER TWO TOURS IN COUNTRY, THE SECOND AS A SNIPER AND SCOUT, THAT WAS TO BE EXPECTED.

BUT TEEG HAD NEVER BEEN THE KIND TO BE AFFECTED... BY ANYTHING.

SO HE FIGURED HE'D JUST WALK OUT OF THE JUNGLE AND LEAVE IT ALL BEHIND.

HE FIGURED WRONG.

TEEG...? WHAT'S **WRONG**, BABY?

ARE YOU OKAY...?

YEAH... I'M FINE...

JUST ROLL OVER...

SLEEP SHOULD HAVE BEEN AN ESCAPE, BUT IT WASN'T...

AND HE FOUND HIMSELF DREADING EVEN THE IDEA OF IT.

HE WONDERED IF HE WAS BECOMING A **HEADCASE**, LIKE SO MANY HE'D KNOWN.

LIKE THE KID WHO THOUGHT HIS RIFLE TALKED TO HIM.

OF COURSE, IT **DID** TALK, BUT IT ONLY HAD **ONE THING** TO SAY.

HE WOULD NOT LET HIMSELF BECOME LIKE THAT KID...

JUST THE THOUGHT OF IT WAS LIKE A KNIFE IN HIS MIND.

TEEGAR?

YOU CAN TALK TO ME... YOU **KNOW** THAT, RIGHT?

YOU CAN TELL ME ANY--

-THING...

OH.

HIS WIFE AND TWO KIDS FELT LIKE ALIENS TO HIM.

HE HADN'T EVEN BEEN HOME WHEN THE BABY WAS BORN SIX MONTHS EARLIER.

AND HE ONLY VAGUELY REMEMBERED THE NIGHT HE'D BEEN CONCEIVED. THE LAST NIGHT OF HIS LEAVE THE PREVIOUS YEAR.

WHEN HE LAY IN BED, NOT SLEEPING, HE COULD FEEL THEM ALL BREATHING IN THE HOUSE AROUND HIM.

IT WAS TOO LOUD. TOO MUCH.

SOME OF THE GUYS OVER THERE LOST THEMSELVES IN WEED OR DOPE...

TEEG! OVER HERE!

WILLY... YOU *STILL* DRINKIN' IN THIS DIVE?

SHIT, NOWHERE ELSE WILL *HAVE ME.*

BUT THAT WASN'T TEEG'S THING.

WELL THEN, FUCK IT... NEXT ROUND'S ON *UNCLE SCAM.*

HE HAD OTHER PATHS TO OBLIVION.

CHRIST, MAN, TAKE IT *EASY*... IT'S EARLY STILL.

DON'T BE SUCH A PUSSY.

OR SOMETHING CLOSE TO IT.

NO! *SERIOUS*... I'S *READY* TA CUT OFF MY TOE...

AIN'T *MY* FUCKIN' WAR...

--SON OF A BITCH!

YOU *FUCKFACE!*

WHUKK

DON'T *EVER* TOUCH ME...

--HEAR BARBER'S LOOKIN' FOR YER ASS ALREADY...

sssnnnnnfff

BARBER? FUCK HIM...

I BLED FER MY COUNTRY...

DOUBT HE THINKS A' THAT AS *HIS* PROBLEM.

OH YEAH, BABY! OH YEAH!

FUCK ME HARDER!

FUCK ME!

--AND GET YOUR FRIEND AND GET THE *FUCK* OUT. *NOW.*

--*SHIT!* BROKE MY FUCKING *FINGER!*

THAT *AIN'T* GOOD, LAWLESS...

ALREADY *OWE* MR BARBER. NOW YER *DAMAGIN'* HIS PROPERTY!

KRAKK

AHH!

AH... FUCKIN' HELL...

SEE, WHEN YOU LEFT TO GO OVER THERE AN' KILL COMMIES AN' WHATNOT...

YOU DIDN'T WALK AWAY WITH NO *CLEAN SLATE*, LAWLESS.

YOU WALKED AWAY OWIN' MR. BARBER *TWO GRAND*.

YEAH, MOTHERFUCKER!

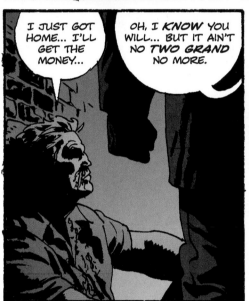

I JUST GOT HOME... I'LL GET THE MONEY...

OH, I *KNOW* YOU WILL... BUT IT AIN'T NO *TWO GRAND* NO MORE.

SEE, WE LEFT THE VIG RUNNING ON *LOW* WHEN YOU WAS OVER IN THE SHIT...

BUT IT'S BEEN A *FEW YEARS*, LAWLESS...

...AN' WEEKLY INTEREST, THAT'S A *REAL BITCH*.

HOW *MUCH*? HOW MUCH IS IT?

FIFTEEN.

FUCK.

BUT WE'RE GONNA MAKE A SPECIAL DEAL, JUST *THIS ONCE*, 'CUZ YER A *WAR HERO* AN' ALL.

YOU GOT EXACTLY *TWO WEEKS* TO PAY... IN FULL.

WHAT'S SO *SPECIAL* ABOUT THAT?

OH YEAH, I LEFT OUT THAT PART... SEE, YOU PAY UP --

--AN' WE *DON'T* KILL YER KIDS!

UHNN!

YOU STUPID PIECE OF SHIT...

BARBER RAN AN UNDERGROUND CASINO DOWNTOWN, WHICH IS HOW TEEG CAME TO OWE HIM SO MUCH MONEY.

BARBER WASN'T SOMEONE TEEG COULD TAKE ON. NO WAY IN HELL.

...UHNN... FUCKIN' BASTARDS...

AND IF HE WAS THREATENING TEEG'S KIDS, IT WAS MORE A *PROMISE* THAN A THREAT.

...WHERE THE FUCK AM I...?

OVER THE NEXT FEW DAYS, TEEG AND WILLY TOOK DOWN A FEW WEAK SCORES.

LIQUOR STORES.

GAS STATIONS.

NOTHING JOBS THAT BARELY BROUGHT IN A FEW HUNDRED BUCKS.

TEEG COULD FEEL THE CLOCK TICKING. HE NEEDED SOMETHING *REAL.*

BUT THE PROBLEM WAS, HE'D *NEVER* BEEN A PLANNER.

HE WAS USUALLY BROUGHT INTO A JOB WHEN IT WAS PRIMED AND READY.

AND FINDING WORK LIKE THAT, AFTER ALL HIS TIME AWAY, WOULDN'T BE EASY.

BUT THEN, NOTHING WAS EASY ANYMORE...

--GONE ALL *HOURS* OF THE DAY *AND* NIGHT!

AND I'M *SURE* I DON'T WANT TO *KNOW* WHERE YOU'VE *BEEN!*

WHAT YOU'VE *BEEN DOING!*

ASSUMING YOU EVEN *KNOW!*

SHUT UP! JUST SHUT UP!

AFTERWARDS, HE'D CURSE HIMSELF FOR FIGHTING IN FRONT OF THE KID.

BUT IN THE HEAT OF THE MOMENT... IN THE HEAT OF ANGER...

...TEEG WAS NEVER THAT BIG ON SELF-CONTROL.

STILL, HIS REPUTATION FOR VIOLENCE WASN'T *ALWAYS* FROWNED ON...

WAY I HEAR IT, YOU TWO'RE LOOKIN' FOR A *MAJOR* SCORE.

AND WHERE'D YOU HEAR *THAT*, HAMSUNN?

SIT BEHIND THIS BAR *TWO HOURS*, YOU'LL HEAR EVERYTHING GOIN' ON IN THIS WHOLE CITY.

NOW, YOU AN' YOUR PAL WANNA HEAR ABOUT A *REAL PAYDAY*?

OR SHOULD I JUST KICK YER ASSES *OUTTA* HERE?

HAMSUNN, THE OWNER OF THE UNDERTOW, WAS AN EX-THIEF, BUT TEEG KNEW NO GOOD THIEF EVER *REALLY* RETIRED.

OKAY, LET'S HEAR IT.

SO HE LAID IT OUT... KEEPING THE DETAILS SUFFICIENTLY VAGUE.

THE TARGET WAS A UNIT IN AN APARTMENT BUILDING, WHERE ONCE A WEEK, DIRTY MONEY WAS COUNTED FOR PICK-UP.

AN EASY FIFTY GRAND OR MORE... AT LEAST.

IT'S SO EASY, WHY NOT JUST GRAB IT YOURSELF?

NAH, I'M WAY PAST PRIME FOR A STICK-UP, TEEG.

I JUST WANT A FAIR *STAKE*. LIKE TWENTY-FIVE PERCENT.

UH HUNH... AND JUST WHOSE MONEY IS THIS?

AH... JUST A BUNCHA *MEXICANS*, TRYIN' TA MUSCLE IN.

ALL RIGHT, FUCK IT... WHEN AND *WHERE*?

STILL WAITIN' ON THE FINAL DETAILS... SHOULD KNOW IN A FEW DAYS.

I'LL HAVE *MY GIRL* HERE CONTACT YOU...

I'M DANICA... NICE TO MEET YOU.

WHATEVER YOU *SAY*, GIRL.

OOH... I LIKE TO HEAR *THAT*, BABY...

HAMSUNN, HE COULD HANDLE... BUT THE GIRL WAS GOING TO BE TROUBLE, OF SOME KIND.

TEEG COULD TELL THAT JUST FROM LOOKING AT HER.

STILL, HE NEEDED A WAY OUT FROM UNDER.

THERE WAS BARELY A WEEK UNTIL BARBER'S MEN WOULD COME TO COLLECT.

...AN' THE AIRPLANE GOES ZOOM...

ZOOM... ZOOM... ZOOM...

...AND THEN THE SOLDIERS DIVE TO THE RESCUE...

...AND GO BOOM BOOM BOOM...

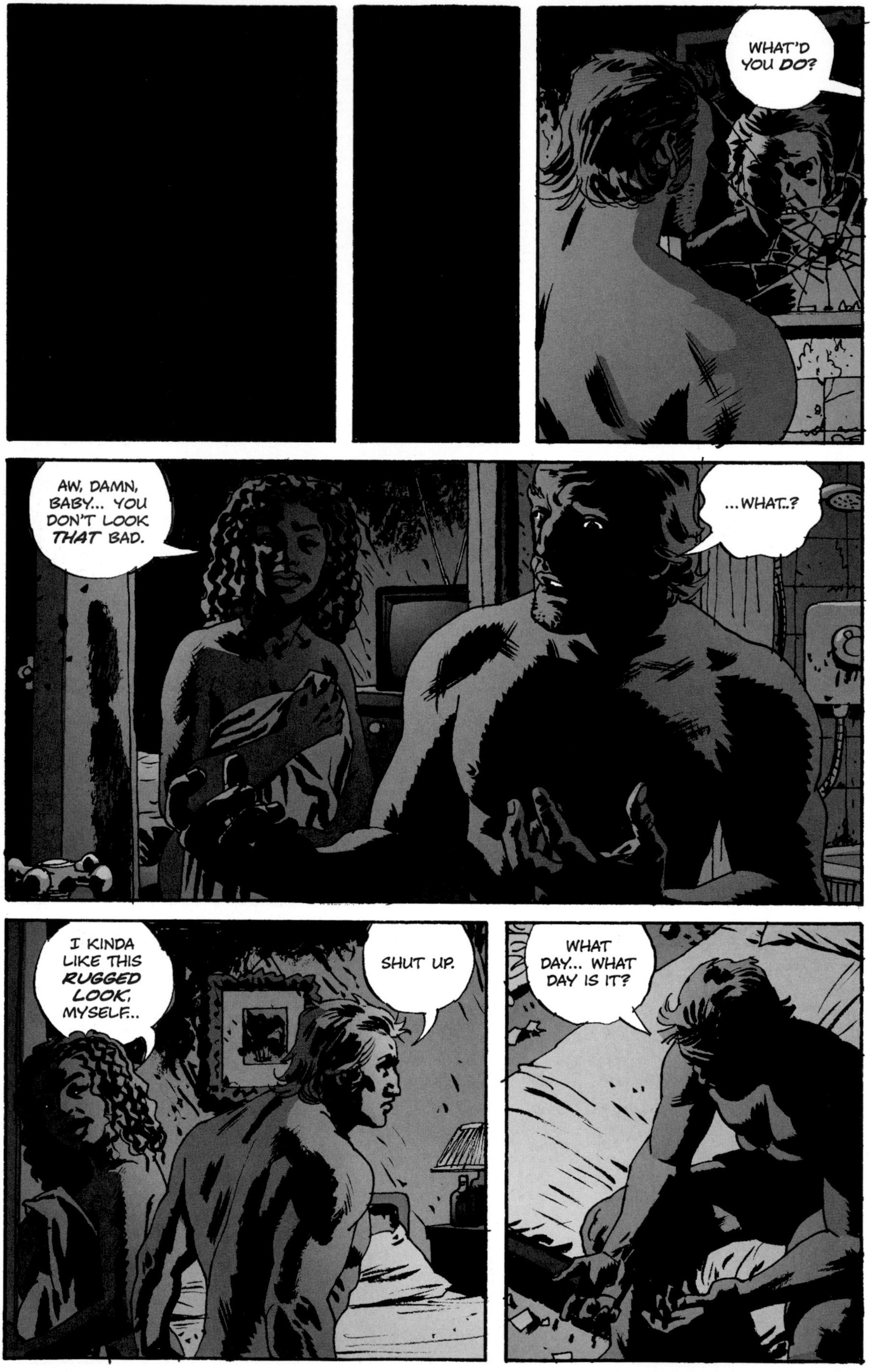
WHAT'D YOU *DO*?
AW, DAMN, BABY... YOU DON'T LOOK *THAT* BAD.
...WHAT..?
I KINDA LIKE THIS *RUGGED LOOK*, MYSELF...
SHUT UP.
WHAT DAY... WHAT DAY IS IT?

THURSDAY, SUGAR... DON'T WORRY... THERE'S STILL TWO DAYS LEFT.

THURSDAY... I WAS... I WAS...

YOU WAS CELEBRATIN' HAMSUNN FINALLY GETTING THE *DETAILS* FOR YOUR SCORE.

AN' I WAS *HELPIN'* YOU.

YEAH... OKAY... YOU MIGHT HAVE'TA REFRESH MY MEMORY A LITTLE.

OHH, *BABY*... I GOT *NO PROBLEM* WITH THAT.

THE DETAILS COME BACK TO HIM LIKE RAZOR SLICES OF TIME.

MEETING HAMSUNN'S GIRL ON THE STREET.

THE LITTLE ROOM AT THE RED ROBIN INN.

AND HER PLAN -- A SIDE DEAL, JUST BETWEEN THEM.

--JUST AN OLD MAN... I CAN'T GET NOWHERE WITH HIM.

BUT WITH A MAN LIKE *YOU*...

A GIRL COULD *GO* PLACES... GET OUT IN THE WORLD...

WHO SAYS I WANNA *LEAVE*?

SHIT, EVERYTHING *ABOUT YOU* SAYS THAT.

YOU'RE A TIGER IN A CAGE... GOT TO BE FREE.

I WON'T CHEAT WILLY OUT OF HIS SHARE...

BUT HAMSUNN, I GOT NO PROBLEM SCREWING HIM.

OKAY, SO WILLY GETS HIS SPLIT, AND *THEN* WE HEAD OUT.

I DON'T KNOW.

IT DON'T HAVE TO BE PERMANENT.

BUT YOU AN' ME... WE CAN HAVE SOME *FUN.*

FOR A WHILE.

TWO DAYS LATER, DANICA'S IDEA ISN'T SEEMING SO BAD.

MAYBE AN ESCAPE IS WHAT HE NEEDS.

MAYBE LETTING THIS CRAZY CHICK USE HIM AS HER WAY OUT WILL BE *HIS*, TOO.

ONCE HE PAYS BARBER OFF, AND IT'S SAFE TO GO.

HNNK HNKK

TEEG? YOU'RE GOING OUT *NOW*?

I WAS JUST ABOUT TO MAKE DINNER...

IT'S BUSINESS.

JUST FOR ONCE CAN'T WE –

CHRIST, WOULD YOU STOP *NAGGIN'* ME?

I *SAID*, IT'S BUSINESS.

THE APARTMENT WAS ON THE THIRD FLOOR.

AND IT WASN'T GUARDED.

KRAKK

NOT ON THE OUTSIDE, AT LEAST.

WHAT THE FUCK ARE YOU --

BLAM BLAM

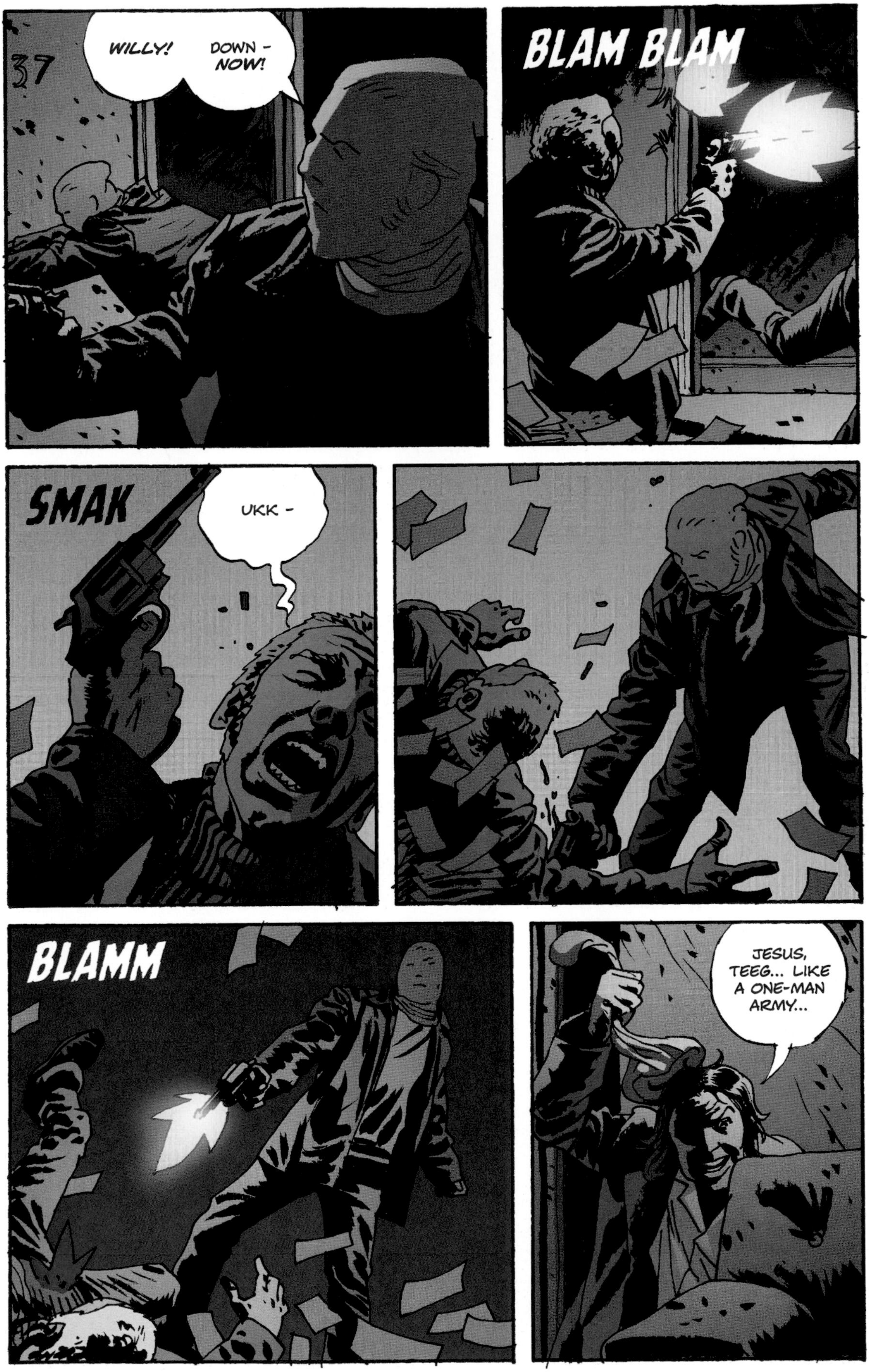
37
WILLY!
DOWN - NOW!
BLAM BLAM
SMAK
UKK -
BLAMM
JESUS, TEEG... LIKE A ONE-MAN ARMY...

WHAT IS IT? WHAT'S **WRONG**?

I DON'T **KNOW**...

...BUT DO THESE GUYS LOOK **MEXICAN** TO YOU?

FUCK, MAN... WHO **GIVES** A SHIT?

LONG AS THEIR MONEY AIN'T PESOS.

AND THE TAKE IS BIG — **FIFTY SEVEN LARGE.**

IN HIS GUT, THOUGH, HE ALREADY KNOWS HE'S MADE A MISTAKE.

HE JUST DOESN'T KNOW HOW BIG UNTIL THE NEXT DAY...

UHT UH... **NO WAY.**

YOU AIN'T PAYIN' ME BACK WITH THAT.

YOU GOT A PROBLEM WITH **CASH** NOW, BARBER?

I GOT A PROBLEM WITH **THAT** CASH... YEAH.

MUST'A BEEN BURIED IN A *BOTTLE*, OR YOU'D'A HEARD THE HYDES GOT *HIT* YESTERDAY.

THE *HYDES*?

NO... *FUCK* NO.

JESUS... DON'T YA EVEN CHECK WHOSE MONEY YOU'RE *STEALIN'* ANYMORE, LAWLESS?

THEY HAD STOLEN THE HYDES' MONEY? WHAT THE HELL WAS HAMSUNN THINKING?

WALTER HYDE HAD BEEN THE TOP DOG IN THE CITY SINCE THE FIFTIES, AND YOU DIDN'T CROSS HIM.

BUT SOME SNIFFING AROUND LED TO WALTER'S SON, SEBASTIAN, WHO WAS TAKING OVER PARTS OF THE BUSINESS. IT WAS *HIS* STASH THEY'D HIT...

...AND MAYBE THE SON WOULD BE EASIER TO DEAL WITH THAN THE FATHER.

HE'S CLEAN, MR HYDE.

ALL RIGHT, THEN... LET'S TALK.

I WANNA GIVE IT BACK... THE MONEY.

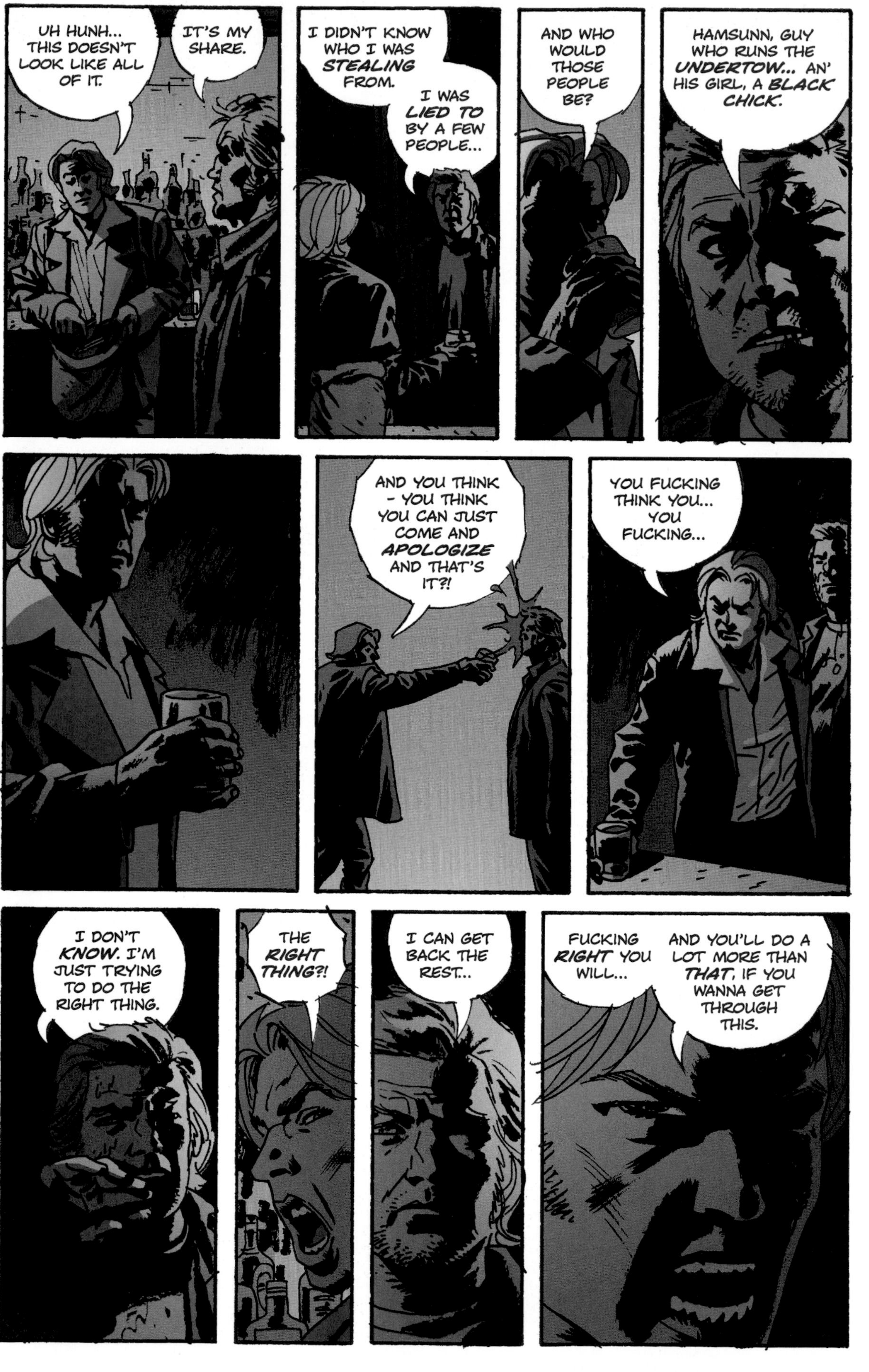
UH HUNH... THIS DOESN'T LOOK LIKE ALL OF IT.
IT'S MY SHARE.
I DIDN'T KNOW WHO I WAS STEALING FROM.
I WAS LIED TO BY A FEW PEOPLE...
AND WHO WOULD THOSE PEOPLE BE?
HAMSUNN, GUY WHO RUNS THE UNDERTOW... AN' HIS GIRL, A BLACK CHICK.
AND YOU THINK - YOU THINK YOU CAN JUST COME AND APOLOGIZE AND THAT'S IT?!
YOU FUCKING THINK YOU... YOU FUCKING...
I DON'T KNOW. I'M JUST TRYING TO DO THE RIGHT THING.
THE RIGHT THING?!
I CAN GET BACK THE REST...
FUCKING RIGHT YOU WILL...
AND YOU'LL DO A LOT MORE THAN THAT, IF YOU WANNA GET THROUGH THIS.

HE DIDN'T REMEMBER WHEN THE DRINKING STARTED THAT DAY.

JUST THAT HE KNEW WHAT HE HAD TO DO TO SURVIVE.

HE DIDN'T REMEMBER TYING HAMSUNN TO THE CHAIR.

I'M TELLIN' YA, TEEG — I DIDN'T KNOW!

BUT HE REMEMBERED THE SUITCASE NEAR THE DOOR, LIKE HE WAS ON HIS WAY OUT OF TOWN.

WHAT CAME NEXT WAS EASY.

KNNCH

AKK--

POKKK

JUST LIKE PULLING A TRIGGER.

HNNK HNK

GET IN.

THIS A NEW CAR?

NEW TO ME. THOUGHT WE NEEDED A GOOD RIDE IF WE WERE LEAVIN'...

WELL, I STILL GOTTA PICK UP MY STUFF...

BUT YOU GOT THE MONEY, RIGHT?

IT'S BACK AT THE HOTEL.

ONLY TAKE A MINUTE TO GET IT, THOUGH, AN' GRAB MY THINGS.

MAN, YOU REALLY IN A HURRY TO SPLIT NOW.

I GUESS... GRAB ME MY SMOKES, WOULD'JA?

THEY'RE IN THE GLOVE BOX.

NO CIGARETTES IN HERE, MAN... JUST A PINT OF SOMETHIN'...

YOU SURE ABOUT --

HYDE WAS VERY SPECIFIC ABOUT WHAT WAS TO BE DONE WITH THE GIRL.

WHERE SHE WAS TO BE LEFT.

SO TEEG FIGURED SHE GOT WHAT SHE DESERVED.

SOMETIMES PEOPLE DO DESERVE IT, HE THOUGHT.

BUT MOST TIMES, IT HAPPENS JUST BECAUSE...

HEY, TEEG, WHAT'S THE *DEAL*, MAN?

I'M HEARIN' MAYBE WE HIT THE *WRONG PLACE*.

YEAH... YEAH, WE *DID*. BUT I'M FIXING IT.

HEY - HEY, MAN!

WHAT THE *FUCK*?!

TEEG -- WE'RE *FRIENDS*!

I KNOW... BUT THIS IS THE ONLY WAY.

BLAM

...FUCKIN' WILLY...

NOW, WHERE THE HELL DID YOU HIDE YOUR END...?

HYDE JR SEEMED SURPRISED TO SEE HIM SO SOON...

THIS *ALL* OF IT, THIS TIME? NOT HOLDING ANY BACK?

I DIDN'T COUNT IT, BUT THAT'S ALL THEY HAD.

AND EVERYTHING *ELSE* WENT JUST LIKE WE SAID?

YEAH. YOUR *MESSAGE* WAS SENT. *LOUD AND CLEAR.*

IS THAT A *TONE* YOU'RE TAKIN' WITH MR HYDE?

YOU *DON'T* WANNA BE TAKIN' NO TONE, GUY.

LEAVE THE MAN ALONE, BRUNO.

HE DOESN'T SCARE.

DO YOU, LAWLESS?

I'VE BEEN SCARED BEFORE...

SO, ARE WE EVEN?

MOSTLY. I'LL FORGET ABOUT MY MEN THAT YOU ACED...

...SINCE THEY CLEARLY WEREN'T WORTH WHAT I WAS PAYIN' THEM.

BUT I TALKED TO BARBER FOR YOU...

HE'S GONNA DROP MOST OF HIS INTEREST AND LET YOU PAY HIM OFF SLOW.

I DIDN'T ASK YOU TO DO THAT.

WAS THAT A THANK YOU?

I DON'T NEED ANY MORE DEBTS.

SHIT. CONSIDER IT A FAVOR THEN, LAWLESS... 'CAUSE I LIKE THE WORK YOU DO.

SO, Y'KNOW... DON'T BE A STRANGER.

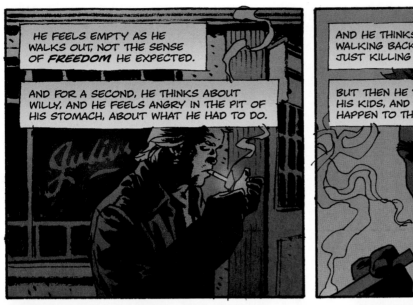

HE FEELS EMPTY AS HE WALKS OUT, NOT THE SENSE OF *FREEDOM* HE EXPECTED.

AND FOR A SECOND, HE THINKS ABOUT WILLY, AND HE FEELS ANGRY IN THE PIT OF HIS STOMACH, ABOUT WHAT HE HAD TO DO.

AND HE THINKS ABOUT WALKING BACK IN THERE AND JUST KILLING THEM ALL.

BUT THEN HE THINKS ABOUT HIS KIDS, AND WHAT WOULD HAPPEN TO THEM IF HE DID.

AND SOMETHING HAPPENS THEN, WHEN HE REMEMBERS HIS SONS, AND THINKS OF THEIR INNOCENT EYES.

A HORROR SWEEPS THROUGH HIM.

A FATHER'S FEAR AND PROTECTIVENESS.

A LOVE FOR HIS SONS THAT HURTS HIM INSIDE.

EVENTUALLY, HE'LL LEARN TO HATE THEM FOR THAT.

BUT IT'LL TAKE A FEW YEARS.

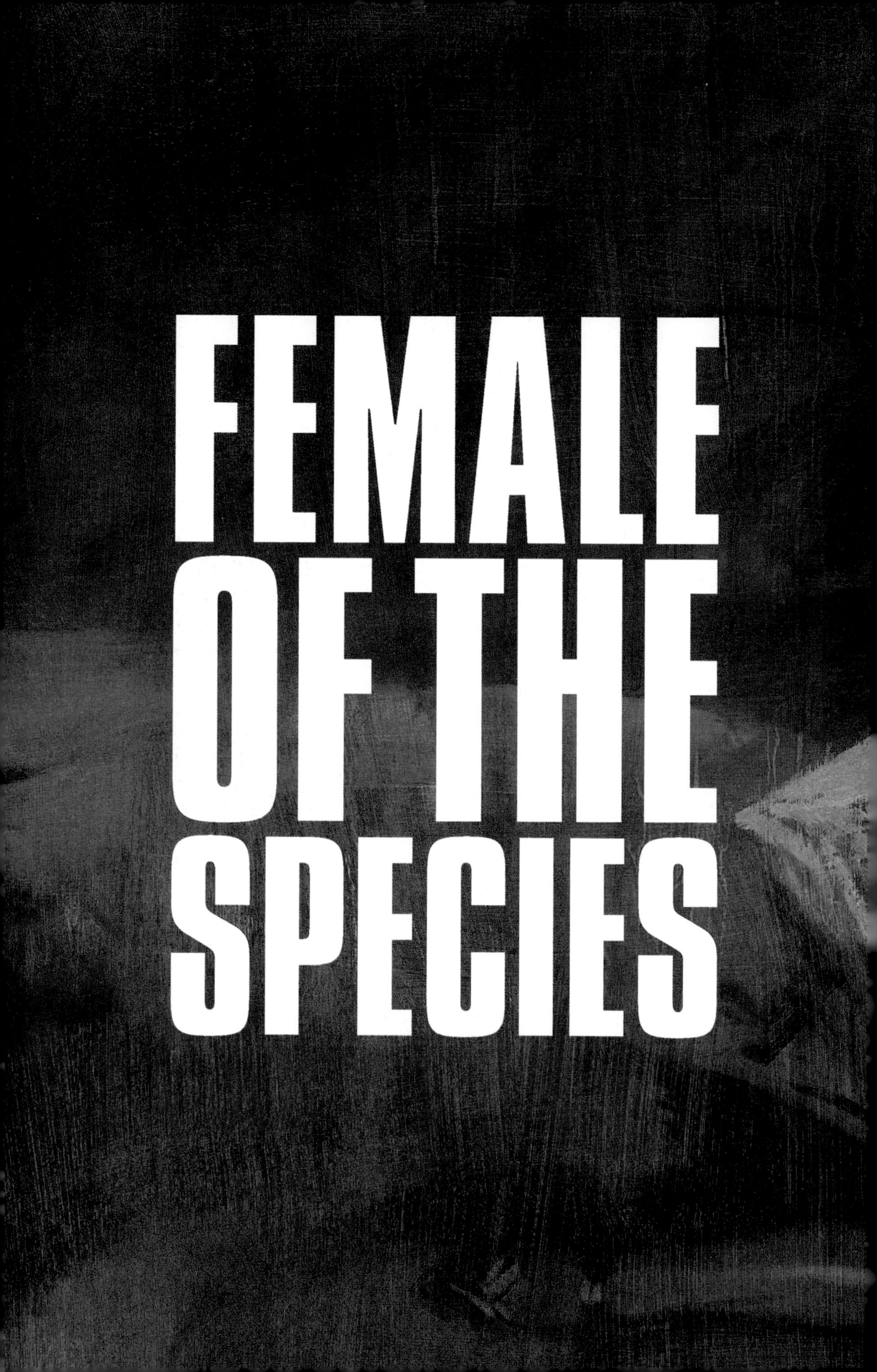

FEMALE OF THE SPECIES

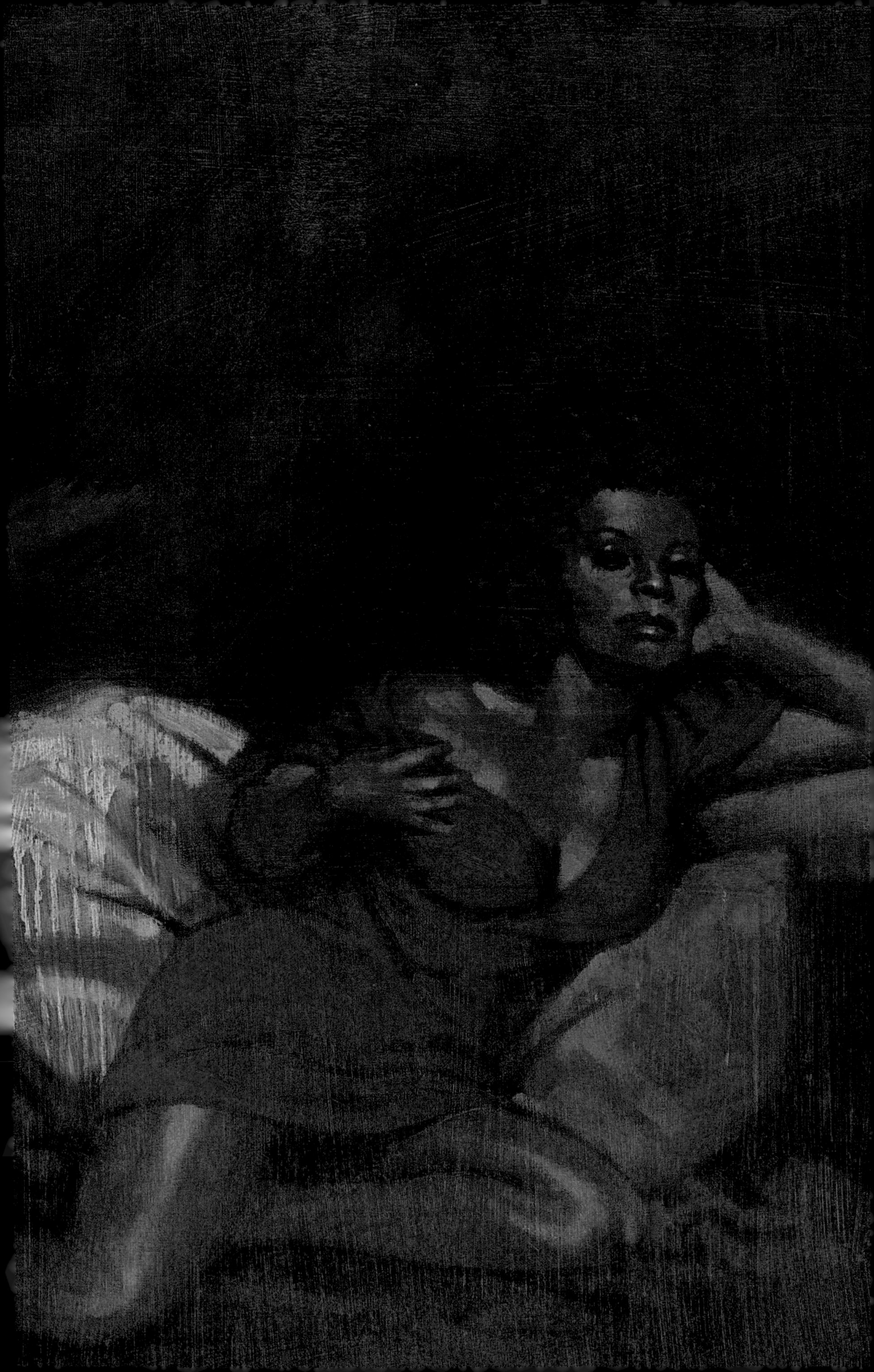

TWO HUNDRED MILES FROM HOME, I'M PRETTY SURE THIS GUY'S GOING TO BE TROUBLE.

TROUBLE I CAN HANDLE, BUT TROUBLE.

FIGURED HIM FOR THE NERVOUS TYPE, THE HOPEFUL TYPE...

KIND YOU SHOW A LITTLE LEG, AND SHAKE A LITTLE ASS, AND THEY DO WHATEVER YOU WANT.

BUT A FEW HOURS INTO THE RIDE, AND HE'S GROWING HIS BALLS BACK.

HENHH... HEHH...?

STOP UP AHEAD, WOULD YA?

I NEED TO USE THE *LADIES ROOM.*

SHOULDN'T BE DOING THIS, I KNOW... NOT WITH *FAT ASS* OUT THERE TO DEAL WITH.

BUT A LITTLE SMACK JUST TAKES THE EDGE OFF.

AND LIFE'S GOT TOO DAMN MANY EDGES.

BUT *GODDAMN*, DOES THIS MAKE THEM ALL BETTER... I'LL NEVER GET OVER THAT.

EVERY SINGLE TIME... JUST MAKES IT *ALL* GO AWAY...

MAKES *ME* GO AWAY...

EVEN THE FIRST TIME, WHEN I DIDN'T KNOW WHAT WAS HAPPENING, BACK IN 1967...

YOU DANICA?

UH... YEAH.

WHAT'S GOIN' ON? WHERE'S SEBASTIAN?

BOYFRIEND'S GOT BUSINESS TO TAKE CARE OF... COULDN'T MAKE IT...

SENT ME TO PICK YOU UP, INSTEAD.

HE BE BACK AT THE HOUSE SOON, THOUGH... DON'T YOU WORRY.

AND WHO ARE YOU, EXACTLY?

NAME'S MARVIN... I WORK FOR SEBASTIAN'S DAD.

YOU SEEN ME AROUND BEFORE, AT THE FIGHTS.

OH, YEAH, RIGHT... WITH MR. HYDE.

OKAY.

SO, LET'S GO...

SURE.

I WAS SO NAÏVE BACK THEN.

ACTUALLY THOUGHT IT WAS EXCITING THAT MY MAN HAD SENT A BRUISER LIKE MARVIN TO FETCH ME.

CAR'S BACK THIS WAY...

TAYLOR & GRASSO'S
Since 1948

I KNEW WHAT SEBASTIAN AND HIS FAMILY WERE ABOUT... THE CRIME AND DRUGS.

AND YEAH, THAT GOT ME WET JUST AS MUCH AS HIS PALE SKIN AGAINST MINE DID.

WHAT CAN I SAY? I WAS YOUNG AND STUPID... AND *IN LOVE*, I GUESS.

AT LEAST UNTIL I GOT IN THAT CAR.

WHO'S *THIS?* YOU DIDN'T –

SHUT UP, BITCH!

HEY – HEY!

NO!

SAID SHUT YER *FUCKIN' MOUTH!*

HOLD HER, MAN.

STOP! WHAT'RE YOU DOIN'?!

I'M *SEBASTIAN'S* GIRL!

NOT ANYMORE, YOU AIN'T.

MRRAAAAHHH!

HOLD HER STILL... HOLD HER FUCKIN' STILL...

GET IT DONE, JERRY.

I FELT THE STING OF THE NEEDLE IN MY NECK.

ONE SECOND, COLD TERROR... THE NEXT, NOTHING BUT BLISS.

AND THEN I DIDN'T FEEL ANYTHING AT ALL.

THERE'S SOME PART OF ME THAT NEVER FELT ANYTHING AGAIN.

I HOLD ONTO THAT PART EVERY DAY.

ARE YOU ALL RIGHT?

YOU WERE IN THERE A LONG TIME...

SO I DON'T FORGET.

JUST DRIVE, MAN... DRIVE...

THIS IS BULLSHIT...

SSKKRREEE

ALL RIGHT, ENOUGH PLAYING AROUND.

FAT MAN... YOU JUST WANNA KEEP DRIVIN'...

NO, THAT'S NOT RIGHT... THAT'S JUST NOT *RIGHT*, GIRL...

I WANT *SOMETHING* FOR THIS RIDE...

I DESERVE IT...

YOU ABOUT TO DESERVE A *BULLET*, MOTHERFUCKER.

AIIEE!

NOW DRIVE, LIKE I SAID... I GOT PLACES TO BE THAT *DON'T* INCLUDE YOUR *COCK*.

JESUS! OH MY GOD!

JUST TAKE IT! TAKE THE CAR!

LET ME GO! I'LL JUST GO!

SORRY... BUT THAT *AIN'T* GONNA HAPPEN.

I NEVER LEARNED HOW TO DRIVE.

MY DRESS WAS RUINED. THAT WAS MY FIRST THOUGHT, WHEN I WOKE UP.

MY NEW DRESS... THOUGHT SEBASTIAN WAS GOING TO PROPOSE THAT NIGHT.

SO I WANTED TO LOOK NICE.

SHE'S *AWAKE*, MARVIN.

NOW GET HER OUT OF HERE.

YEAH YEAH... I'LL TELL THE BOSS YOU *FIXED* IT.

...HEY...?

...WHATTA YOU...

...YOU DO TA ME...?

NOTHIN'. JUST TOOK CARE'A YOUR *PROBLEM*...

...BABY.

I DON'T KNOW HOW I GOT HOME AND INTO MY BED.

JUST REMEMBER WAKING UP, LIKE IT'D ALL BEEN SOME BAD DREAM.

...WHAT... WHAT IS...

BUT KNOWING IT WASN'T.

KLIK

MOMMA?

MOMMA... PLEASE WAKE UP...

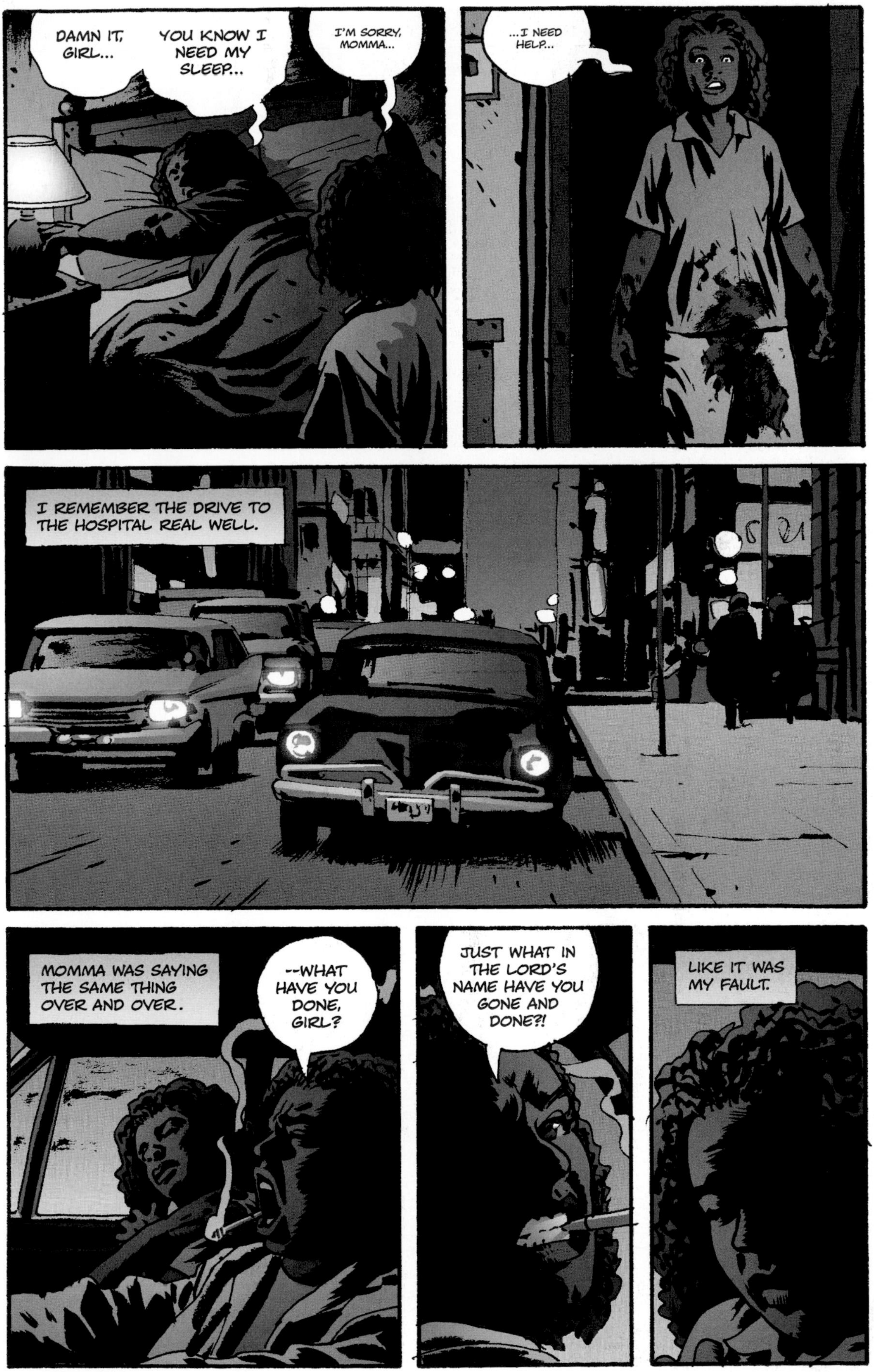
DAMN IT, GIRL...
YOU KNOW I NEED MY SLEEP...
I'M SORRY, MOMMA...
...I NEED HELP...
I REMEMBER THE DRIVE TO THE HOSPITAL REAL WELL.
MOMMA WAS SAYING THE SAME THING OVER AND OVER.
--WHAT HAVE YOU DONE, GIRL?
JUST WHAT IN THE LORD'S NAME HAVE YOU GONE AND DONE?!
LIKE IT WAS MY FAULT.

AND MAYBE SHE WAS RIGHT. MAYBE IT WAS.

I WAS THE ONE WHO PICKED SEBASTIAN OVER HIS FRIEND, JAKE.

JAKE THE BOXER. HE WAS THE ONE I LIKED FIRST.

BUT THERE WAS A MOMENT WHEN IT FELT LIKE JAKE *WANTED ME* TO PICK SEBASTIAN.

HE'S A GOOD GUY.

LIKE HE WAS TRYING TO GIVE AWAY WHAT WASN'T HIS TO GIVE.

NOT LIKE THE *OTHER* WHITE BOYS.

UH HUNH...

SO I RUBBED HIS FACE IN THAT...

...AND I PICKED WRONG.

WOW... YOU ARE WILD, BABY.

SO WRONG I DON'T THINK I'VE EVER BEEN RIGHT AGAIN.

BUT THERE WAS SOMETHING REAL THERE, TOO. I KNOW THAT.

YOUNG AND IN LOVE WAS *REAL*.

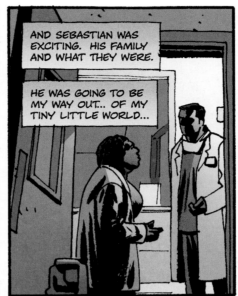

AND SEBASTIAN WAS EXCITING. HIS FAMILY AND WHAT THEY WERE.

HE WAS GOING TO BE MY WAY OUT... OF MY TINY LITTLE WORLD...

MAYBE OF THIS WHOLE FUCKED-UP CITY.

AND IN A WAY HE STILL WAS.

DON'T, DANICA... JUST *DON'T*.

'CAUSE AFTER THE DOCTORS TOLD MOMMA *WHY* I ALMOST DIED, SHE WAS SO ASHAMED THAT SHE SENT ME AWAY.

TO MY AUNT'S PLACE IN CENTER CITY.

MY AUNT JEANNIE, WHO COULDN'T CARE IF I LIVED OR DIED...

-AN' YOU BEST NOT BE SMOKIN' *MY* CIGARETTES, GIRL.

...AS LONG AS MY SOUL WAS PLEDGED TO JESUS.

SAY IT, DANICA... TELL *JESUS* YOU WANT HIM IN YOUR LIFE.

BEG THE LORD TO *FORGIVE* YOUR SINFUL WAYS...

BEG HIM TO COME *INTO* *YOUR* HEART...

I DO... I WANT JESUS'S LOVE.

IT WAS AN EASY LIE...

...BECAUSE I KNEW JESUS DIDN'T WANT ME ANYMORE THAN I WANTED HIM.

I JUST WANTED TO FORGET.

BUT I COULDN'T DO THAT, EITHER.

NOT WITHOUT SOME CHEMICAL HELP, AT LEAST.

FUNNY THAT THE ONLY THING THAT COULD MAKE ME FORGET THOSE MEN'S HANDS ON ME...

...WAS THE SAME THING THEY GAVE ME WHEN THEY TOOK EVERYTHING AWAY.

BUT MAYBE THAT'S JUST MY EXCUSE.

ALL JUNKIES GOTTA HAVE *AT LEAST* ONE OF THOSE.

DON'T YOU TRY ANYTHING, OLD MAN... OR I'LL CUT YOU.

I DON'T WANT NONE'A YOU... JUST WANNA GET HIGH...

ONCE I NODDED MY WAY RIGHT OUT OF THE 11TH GRADE, AUNT JEANNIE REALIZED I'D FOUND MY OWN PATH TO GOD...

YOU'VE BROKEN MY *HEART*, GIRL... MAY *GOD* BE MY WITNESS.

AND SHE PUT MY ASS OUT ON THE STREET... WHERE I BELONGED.

I GAVE THOSE STREETS A LONG COLD LOOK, AND MADE SOME CHOICES.

THE SMACK WASN'T GOIN' AWAY, SO A STRAIGHT JOB WAS OUT.

AND NO WAY WAS I BECOMING A FUCKING HOOKER.

BUT DANCING, THAT I COULD *MAYBE* DO, I FIGURED.

LORNA LARU

BUCK NAKED GIRLS

AND WITH ENOUGH DOPE... I JUST LOST MYSELF UP THERE...

REALLY SOMETHING TO *SEE*... SUPPOSEDLY.

BUT IT WASN'T 'TIL TWO YEARS LATER THAT I FIGURED OUT MY *REAL GIFT*...

I'M GONNA *WATCH YOU* TONIGHT, BABY.

GONNA PRETEND YOU'RE DANCIN' FOR ME.

I *WILL* BE, BABY.

BARRY, THE BOUNCER AT *RUBY'S LEGS*, WAS THE FOURTH MAN I FUCKED... AND I LEARNED A LOT FROM HIM.

LEARNED THAT PUSSY DRIVES MEN CRAZY SOMETIMES.

C'MON BABY... JUST LET ME PUT THE HEAD IN...

...JUST FOR A SECOND...

AND THEY THINK ABOUT IT *A LOT MORE* THAN THEY WANT US TO KNOW.

AW YEAH... AW YEAH...

THAT'S PART OF THE CRAZY.

HOW 'BOUT A PRIVATE DANCE, COCOA?

I DON'T DO THOSE.

A HUNDRED BUCKS... JUST TO *TOUCH* IT.

TOUCH WHAT?

THIS. WHAT ELSE?

YOU DON'T WANNA DO THAT, MAN...

I'M JUST TRYIN' TO BE FRIEN'LY... I GOT MONEY... I --

MOTHERFUCKER!

UK --

STUPID MOTHERFUCKIN' MOTHERFUCKER!

KRAKK

HE WAS SOME BUSINESSMAN, A FRIEND OF THE MAYOR'S...

...AND BARRY NEARLY KILLED HIM.

BUT THAT WAS WHEN I REALIZED SOMETHING... ALL PUSSY MAY DRIVE MEN CRAZY...

BUT *MY* PUSSY WAS A DEADLY WEAPON.

AFTER THAT, THINGS CHANGED.

I STARTED LEARNING HOW TO *CONTROL* THAT POWER.

WENT FROM DANCING EVERY NIGHT TO A ROOMFUL OF MEN... TO *BARELY EVER* DANCING FOR JUST A FEW OF THEM.

AND IT WASN'T ALWAYS SLUMMING. THERE'S SOME FINE-LOOKING RICH MEN IN THIS WORLD...

MEN WHO'LL BUY *HALF* THAT WORLD FOR YOU IF YOU KNOW HOW TO PLAY THEM.

AND THAT'S JUST WHAT I DID FOR A WHILE... I *PLAYED*.

PLAYED THEM AGAINST EACH OTHER.

PLAYED MYSELF INTO THEIR FINANCES.

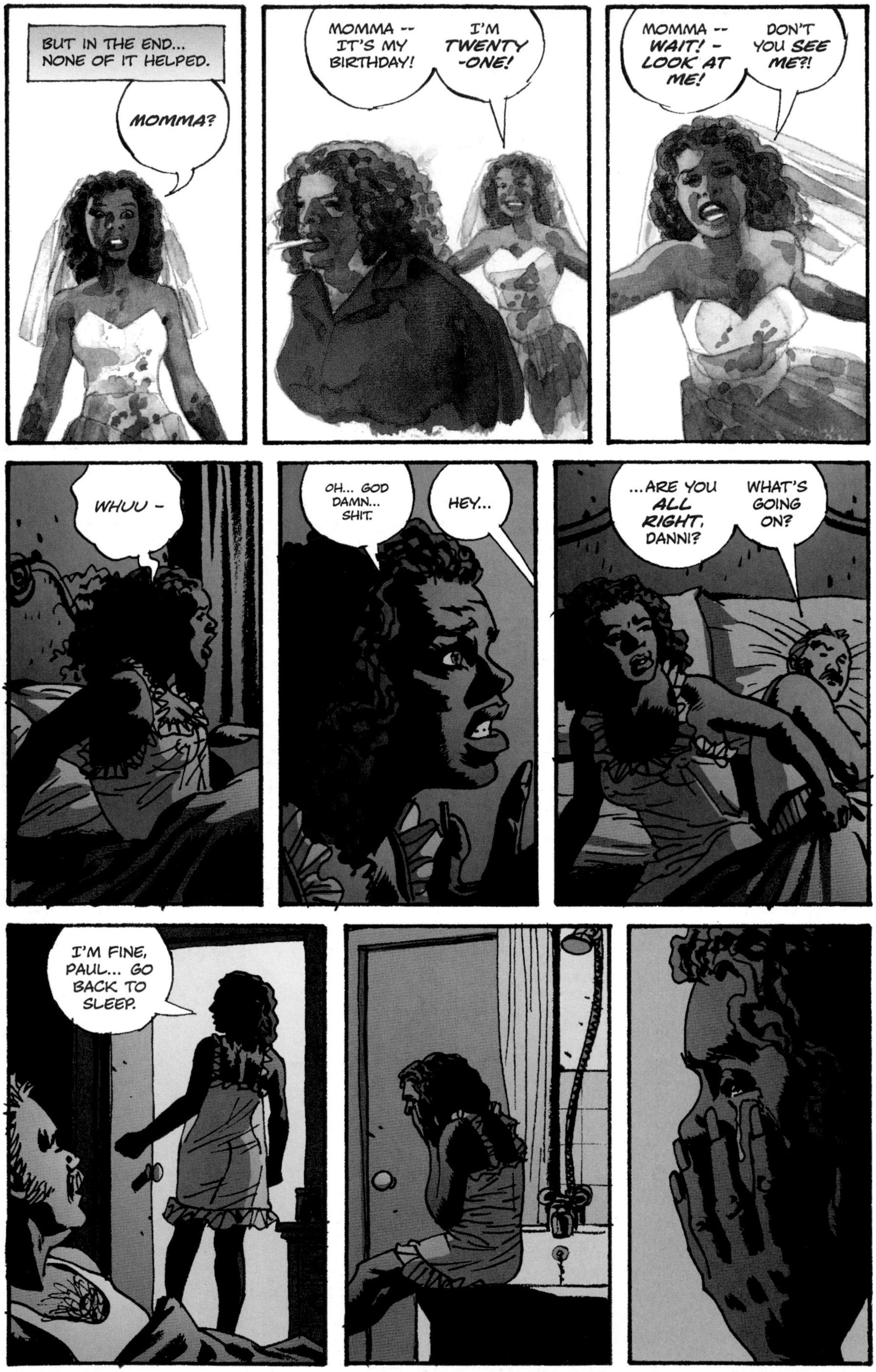
BUT IN THE END... NONE OF IT HELPED.
MOMMA?
MOMMA -- IT'S MY BIRTHDAY!
I'M TWENTY -ONE!
MOMMA -- WAIT! - LOOK AT ME!
DON'T YOU SEE ME?!
WHUU -
OH... GOD DAMN... SHIT.
HEY...
...ARE YOU ALL RIGHT, DANNI?
WHAT'S GOING ON?
I'M FINE, PAUL... GO BACK TO SLEEP.

THE MONEY AND THE HIGH LIFE HAD WEANED ME OFF MY HABIT OVER THE YEARS... BUT I WAS ALWAYS CHIPPIN' A LITTLE.

I'D SHOOT UP BETWEEN MY TOES IN A DRESSING ROOM WHILE SPENDING SOME MAN'S MONEY.

OR DO A LINE BEHIND THE BAR AT SOME CLUB.

AND I'D TELL MYSELF I DIDN'T NEED IT, BUT THAT WAS A LIE.

'CAUSE WHEN I LOOKED IN THE MIRROR, I SAW A GIRL WAY TOO OLD FOR HER YEARS.

SAW A FACE WITH NO JOY.

A SMILE THAT HAD NOTHING LEFT IN IT BUT EMPTY.

IN *HERE*, BABE.

PAUL?

WHAT'RE *YOU* DOING HOME IN THE MIDDLE OF THE DAY?

SIT DOWN.

WHAT IS THIS?

I KNOW *EVERYTHING*, DANNI.

WHAT? EVERYTHING?

WHAT DOES *THAT* MEAN?

I HIRED A DETECTIVE TO FIND OUT ABOUT YOU.

BECAUSE I WANTED TO *MARRY YOU* AND MY PARTNERS... THEY JUST...

I *KNOW*, DANNI...

YEAH... WHAT DO YOU *KNOW?*

I KNOW EVERYTHING!

LOOK – THIS IS YOU AND *TWO* OTHER MEN.

YOU SAW THEM *BOTH* LAST WEEK ON DIFFERENT DAYS.

ARE WE *ALL* PAYING YOUR RENT?

OR ARE YOU JUST TRYING TO GET A PIECE OF MY *BUSINESS?*

LIKE THOSE SHARES OF *NEOCORP* YOU'RE COLLECTING ON.

MY DETECTIVE SAYS THAT STOCK WAS *YOUR PRICE* FOR ENDING AN AFFAIR QUIETLY.

I'M SURE I DON'T EVEN WANT TO *KNOW* WHERE THE REST OF YOUR MONEY COMES FROM.

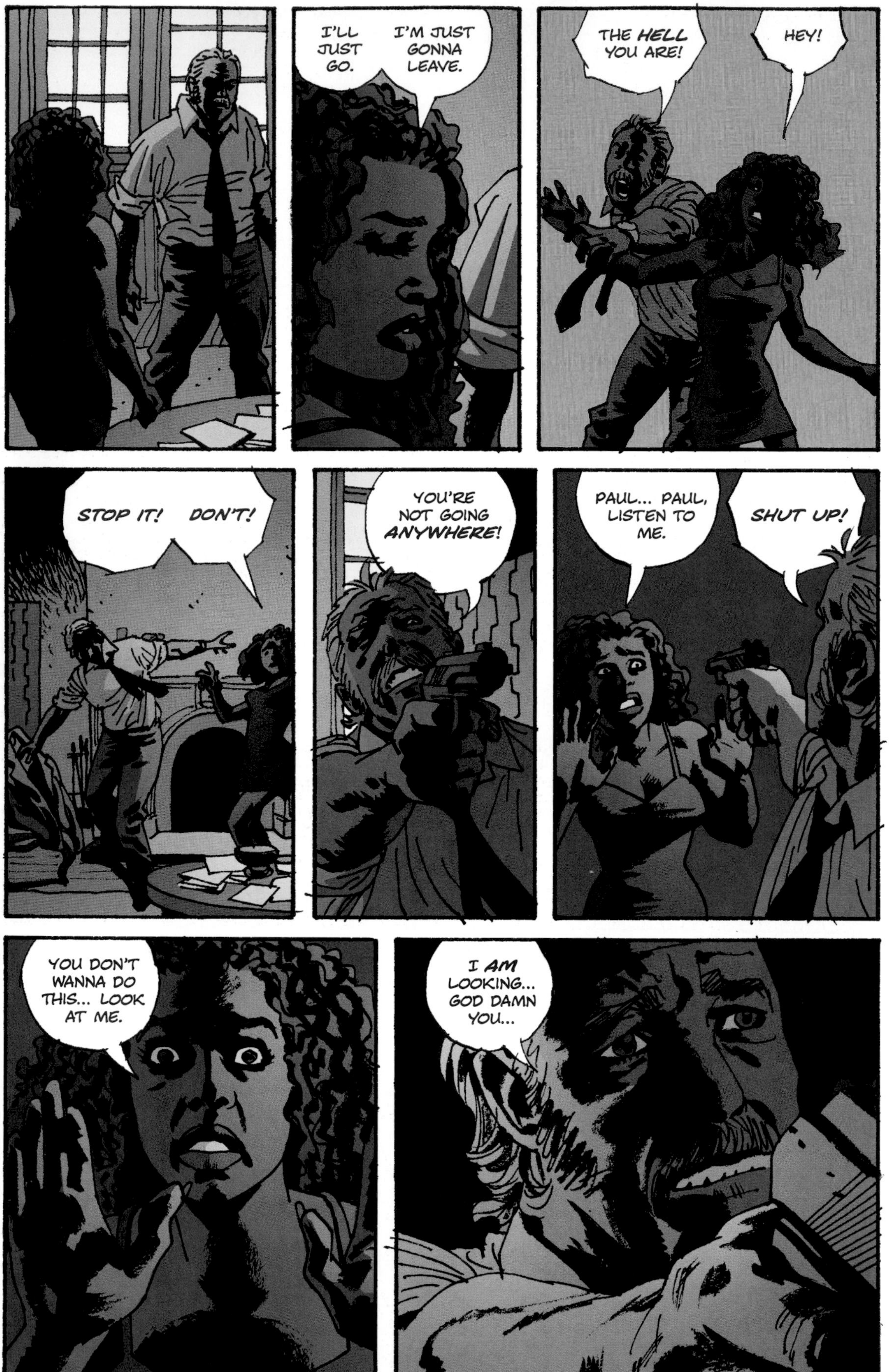
I'LL JUST GO.
I'M JUST GONNA LEAVE.
THE *HELL* YOU ARE!
HEY!
STOP IT!
DON'T!
YOU'RE NOT GOING *ANYWHERE!*
PAUL... PAUL, LISTEN TO ME.
SHUT UP!
YOU DON'T WANNA DO THIS... LOOK AT ME.
I *AM* LOOKING... GOD DAMN YOU...

JESUS, DANNI... DIDN'T YOU CARE ABOUT ME AT ALL?

I LOVED YOU.

AND I DON'T KNOW WHAT MADE THIS TIME DIFFERENT.

DON'T KNOW WHY PAUL'S TEARS REMINDED ME OF POOR JAKE WHEN HE CAME TO SEE ME THAT DAY IN THE HOSPITAL.

DON'T KNOW WHY HIS HEARTBREAK GOT TO ME, AFTER I HAD DESTROYED SO MANY OTHER MEN...

...BUT IT DID.

C'MON, BABY... IT'S OKAY... IT'S OKAY...

I'M SORRY...

WHY...? WHY'D YOU DO THIS TO ME...?

I DON'T KNOW... I'M SORRY...

I WON'T DO IT ANYMORE...

AND I THINK I EVEN MEANT IT.

SOMETHING INSIDE ME WAS SUDDENLY SCREAMING FOR A WAY OUT...

OF WHAT HAD BEEN DONE TO ME... WHAT MY LIFE HAD BECOME...

PAUL COULD TAKE CARE OF ME... HE LOVED ME...

AND HE WAS A GOOD MAN.

IN THE YEAR I'D BEEN SEEING HIM, HE'D BEEN NOTHING BUT TENDER TO ME.

EVEN WHEN HE HAD NO REASON TO BE.

...JUST... PROMISE ME...

I PROMISE.

HE WAS A MAN WHO DESERVED A LOT BETTER THAN I'D GIVEN HIM SO FAR.

WHO DESERVED LOVE.

OH... GOD DAMN IT...

BABE...?

WHAT'RE YOU... DOING?

DANNI? HELLO...?

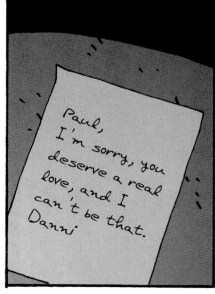

Paul,
I'm sorry, you deserve a real love, and I can't be that.
Danni

I FEEL THE CITY APPROACHING NOW WITH EACH MILE.

LIKE IT'S BEEN CALLING ME BACK HOME ALL THESE YEARS... BUT I COULDN'T HEAR IT UNTIL THIS MORNING.

AND THEN I JUST KNEW THAT THERE WAS NO PLACE ELSE LEFT FOR ME.

NO ESCAPE IN SOME RICH MAN'S LOVING ARMS.

AND IT HURTS, BUT I'M SMILING ANYWAY.

REMEMBERING THAT NAÏVE LITTLE GIRL, SO IMPRESSED BY WHAT'S WRONG WITH THE WORLD.

I CAN ALMOST SEE SEBASTIAN'S FACE, FIVE YEARS OLDER NOW...

CAN ALMOST FEEL HIM INSIDE ME, READY TO GIVE UP ALL HIS SECRETS...

...SO I CAN RUIN *HIM*, THIS TIME.

OVER HERE'S GOOD, MAN.

I CAN JUST WALK FROM —

AHH!

HEY!

DON'T FUCK AROUND — HEY!

BLAM

...SHOT ME... FUCKING SHOT ME...

...SHOT...

FUCKING ASSHOLE. I WAS GETTING OUT.

FUCKIN' MEN IN *CARS*...

I LEAVE THE POOR BASTARD IN HIS MESS... KNOWING I GOT MY *OWN* MESSES TO GO STIR UP.

HELL, MAYBE HE DESERVES IT. MAYBE WE ALL DO.

OR MAYBE HE'S A SIGN OF THINGS TO COME.

'CAUSE WHAT I CAME BACK FOR IS DUMB AND DANGEROUS AND PROBABLY DOOMED.

I FEEL THAT AS SURE AS THE SIDEWALK BENEATH MY FEET.

VIETNAM VET- PLEASE HELP

BUT I'M NOT AFRAID. THIS CITY ALREADY KILLED ME ONCE.

The End

Brubaker Phillips Staples

COLLECTING THE ACCLAIMED COMIC SERIES CRIMINAL

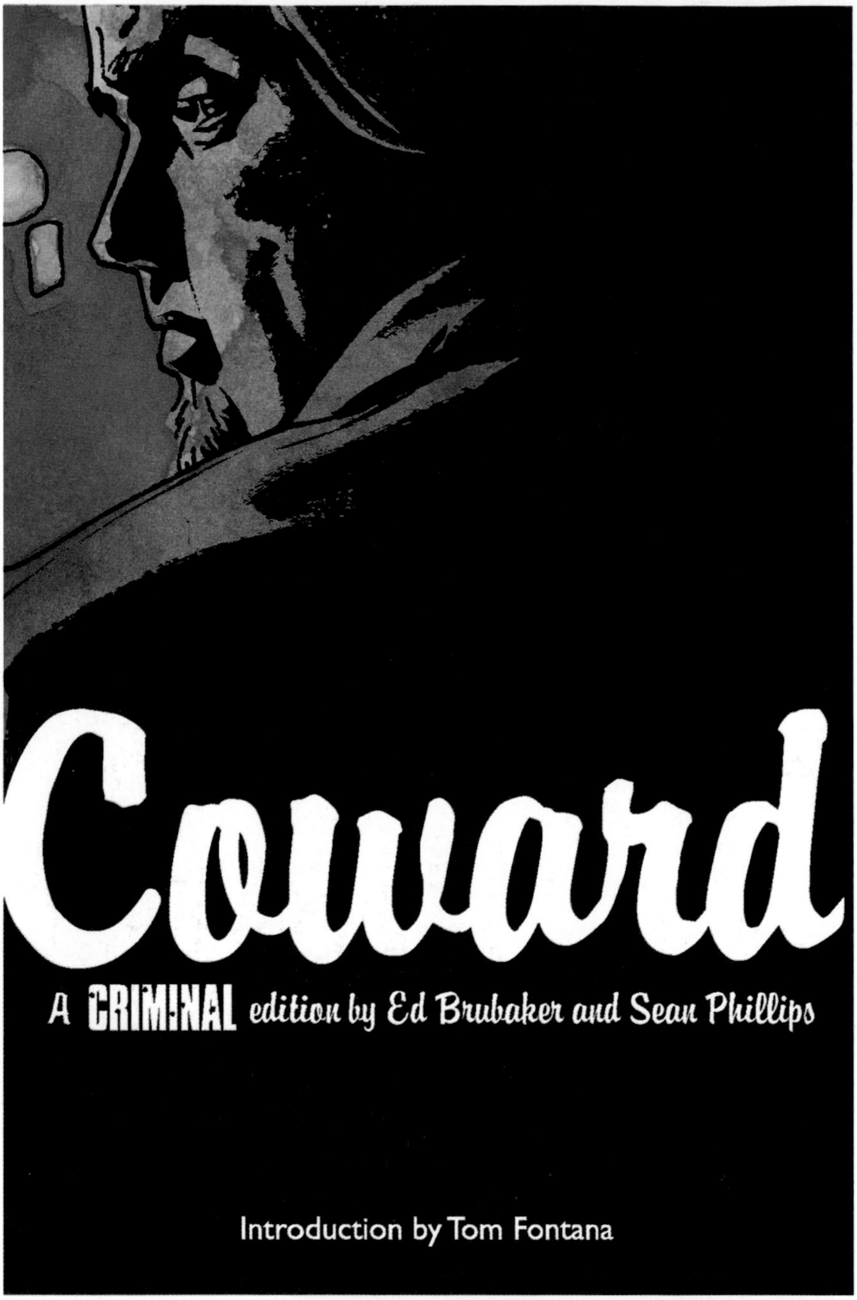
Coward
A CRIMINAL edition by Ed Brubaker and Sean Phillips
Introduction by Tom Fontana

EISNER AWARD WINNER - BEST NEW SERIES and BEST WRITER

HARVEY AWARD WINNER - BEST WRITER

SPIKE TV SCREAM AWARD WINNER - BEST ARTIST

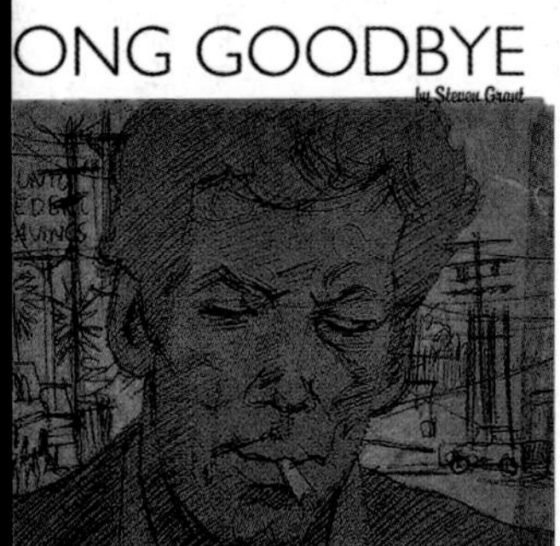
ONG GOODBYE
by Steven Grant

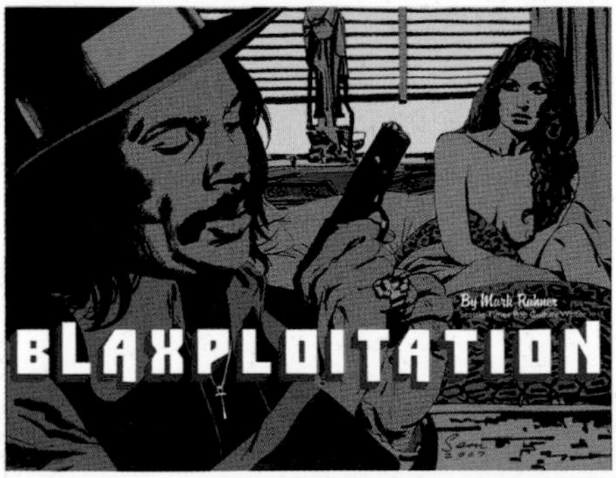
BLAXPLOITATION

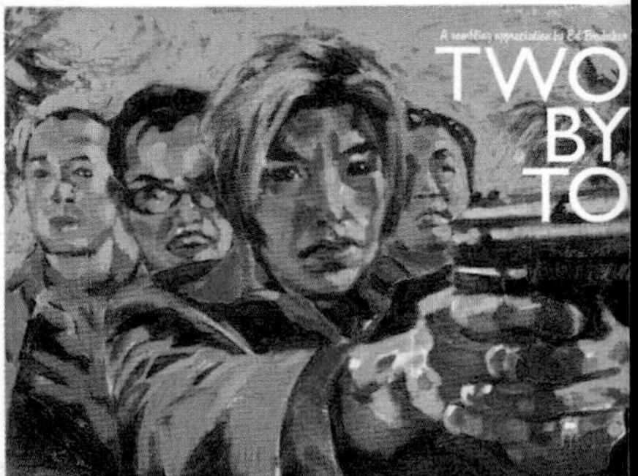
TWO
BY
TO

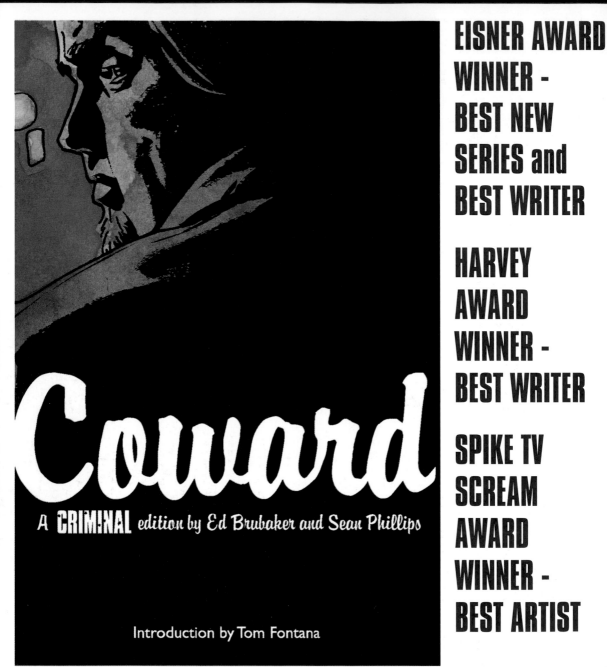

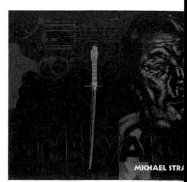